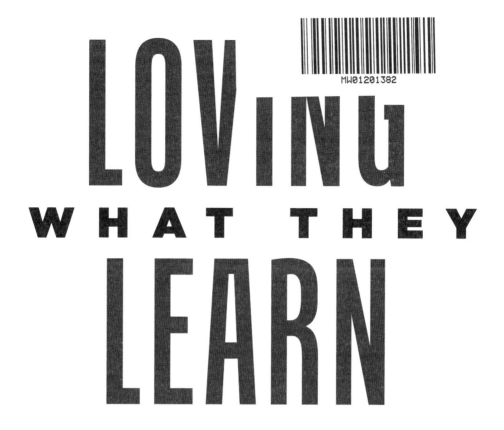

LOVING WHAT THEY LEARN

Research-Based Strategies to Increase Student Engagement

ALEXANDER McNEECE

Solution Tree | Press
a division of
Solution Tree

555 North Morton Street
Bloomington, IN 47404
800.733.6786 (toll free) / 812.336.7700
FAX: 812.336.7790

email: info@SolutionTree.com
SolutionTree.com

Visit **go.SolutionTree.com/instruction** to download the free reproducibles in this book.

Printed in the United States of America

Library of Congress Cataloging-in-Publication Data

Names: McNeece, Alexander, author.
Title: Loving what they learn : research-based strategies to increase
    student engagement / Alexander McNeece.
Description: Bloomington, IN : Solution Tree Press, 2020. | Includes
    bibliographical references and index.
Identifiers: LCCN 2019023593 (print) | LCCN 2019023594 (ebook) | ISBN
    9781949539219 (paperback) | ISBN 9781949539226 (ebook)
Subjects: LCSH: Motivation in education. | Academic achievement. |
    Teacher-student relationships.
Classification: LCC LB1065 .M359 2020 (print) | LCC LB1065 (ebook) | DDC
    370.154--dc23
LC record available at https://lccn.loc.gov/2019023593
LC ebook record available at https://lccn.loc.gov/2019023594

Solution Tree
Jeffrey C. Jones, CEO
Edmund M. Ackerman, President

Solution Tree Press
President and Publisher: Douglas M. Rife
Associate Publisher: Sarah Payne-Mills
Art Director: Rian Anderson
Managing Production Editor: Kendra Slayton
Senior Production Editor: Tonya Maddox Cupp
Content Development Specialist: Amy Rubenstein
Copy Editor: Kate St. Ives
Proofreader: Elisabeth Abrams
Text and Cover Designer: Abigail Bowen
Editorial Assistant: Sarah Ludwig

ACKNOWLEDGMENTS

I extend deep gratitude to all the teachers I work with currently, have met during one of my trainings, and have worked with in the past. So much of this book is a result of what I learned from you. It has been an honor to collaborate with you.

I offer deep appreciation for my wife. Molly is an art teacher, but she is also my first reader. Her insights and responses have made this book better. Given the fact that we are raising children, most of that reading is done late into the evening. She is a constant supporter of my writing.

I want to thank my high school English teachers: Mr. Kelly (summer school), Mr. Moran, Mr. Tenbusch, and Mrs. Barrett. Their patience and dedication helped connect me to writing and the classic literature that grew my academic self-concept and changed my life.

With sincere thankfulness, I must acknowledge the entire Solution Tree team for the help and support in turning this book from a wish to a reality. This includes many people, but I especially need to thank Amy Rubenstein, Claudia Wheatley, Tonya Cupp, and Douglas Rife.

Solution Tree Press would like to thank the following reviewers:

Trevor Goertzen
Associate Principal
Spring Hill Middle School
Spring Hill, Kansas

Sean Maloney
Fourth-Grade Teacher
Brooklyn Elementary School
Brooklyn, Connecticut

Dana Johansen
English Teacher
Greenwich Academy
Greenwich, Connecticut

Lorraine Perez
Science Teacher
Russellville High School
Russellville, Alabama

Visit **go.SolutionTree.com/instruction** to download
the free reproducibles in this book.

TABLE OF CONTENTS

Reproducible pages are in italics.

ABOUT THE AUTHOR

 **Alexander McNeece, PhD,** is director of instructional services and state and federal grants for Garden City School District in Garden City, Michigan. Alexander previously served as a high school football coach, elementary teacher, and middle school English language arts teacher.

Alexander is an active member of the Metro Bureau's Council of Academic Leadership in Michigan, where he has served as a state-level committee liaison. In 2017, with a team of teachers and principals, he presented to the Michigan State Board of Education based on the tremendous early literacy growth the district achieved with the professional learning communities framework. As a consultant, Alexander has worked with districts around the United States and Canada to help close the achievement gap, transform school culture, strengthen the school-improvement process, and develop Unstoppable Learning pedagogy.

He holds both a bachelor's and a master's degree in curriculum and instruction from Michigan State University. In 2017, Alexander earned a doctor of philosophy degree in educational leadership from Eastern Michigan University with his dissertation, "Michigan's Quantitative School Culture Inventories and Student Achievement." He was an award-winning principal at Douglas Elementary School, and has written children's books and *Launching and Consolidating Unstoppable Learning*.

To learn more about Alexander's work, visit www.alexandermcneece.com or follow @AlexMcNeece on Twitter.

To book Alexander McNeece for professional development, contact pd@SolutionTree.com.

INTRODUCTION

From the school's open third-floor window, Alex heard the subtle acceleration of cars starting down 7 Mile Road. He looked out the window. It was a lazy summer day, and the drivers didn't seem to be in a hurry. "Who wants to go to work in the summer?" Alex thought. He made his eyes focus on the blackboard. It was the summer after his eighth-grade year, but Alex's school year had not ended. The high school required him to retake his English class. It was hot, and there was no air conditioning.

Mr. Kelly continued: "This paper has to be typed and double spaced. You just have to pick the book today. We have many you can pick from, all pretty exciting and all classics! OK, class, you have the rest of the hour to pick your novel; get browsing." Some of the books were skinny, but some were thick. Those scared Alex. He looked around. None of the students were quick to stand up and approach the pile of books on the table at the front of the room.

"Come on, come on. They don't bite," Mr. Kelly quipped. Slowly, a few of the students began peeling their bodies from the chairs. Alex stayed in his seat, contemplating sneaking out of the room, but he realized in a panic that the students who had gotten up first were taking all the shorter reads. In a second, Alex was up and quickly moving to the front of the room. His eyes scanned for the slimmest books on the table. He reached out. Topic didn't matter, characters didn't matter, setting didn't matter—he wanted the shortest book he could get. He grabbed what was left and looked at the cover: *The Outsiders* by S.E. Hinton (1967). Alex walked back to his seat as a few of the last students made their selections.

"OK, everyone. This weekend, your homework is to read chapter one and be ready to tell a classmate about it," Mr. Kelly announced. "You can get started quietly reading now." Alex looked down at the book and back up to the front of the room to find Mr. Kelly looking directly at him with the "get-to-work" face. A little surprised, Alex's eyes jumped back down to his book. He opened it to page one. "I hate reading," he thought, and just stared at the first page for the rest of the hour.

• • • • • • • • • • • • • • • ♥ • • • • • • • • • • • • • • •

This story is not fictional. This was *my* experience as a reader. I thought I hated English, books, and writing. I had gotten into a downward cycle of achievement that made me believe that I was not good at those things. Since then, I have been an English teacher, presenter, and author. I'll finish my story of summer-school English class in the epilogue (page 135).

What changed for me? How did I become engaged? I had a variety of positive classroom experiences and influential teachers like the ones I will discuss throughout this book. The academic and personal experiences I share, paired with research and strategies, are the lens I use to explore and help clarify what makes people believe they are skilled or not skilled in a particular area of study or part of life. The related scientifically backed strategies will help you find ways to help students start loving what they learn.

How does that infatuation with academics begin? It begins with engagement.

When you walk through the hallways of your school and peek into classrooms, do you see engagement? Are students active and excited (or immersed and focused), connecting? What are you and your team going to do for those students who are disengaged? Do your colleagues have a sense of collective responsibility, and does everyone share engagement strategies?

To be clear, engaging all students is difficult. It takes knowledge, skills, thoughtfulness, and a team of teachers supporting each other. The tools and materials shared throughout this book are ideal for use as part of a professional learning community (PLC). This book was written to help you and your collaborative team work toward answering the third and fourth critical questions of a professional learning community: "How will we respond when some students do not learn?" and "How will we extend the learning for students who are already proficient?" (DuFour, DuFour, Eaker, Many, & Mattos, 2016, p. 36)? This book's solution is to *engage them*!

Some students come to school already engaged. Other students need more help from us. This book will help both types of students. I think it's important to acknowledge the view some educators have that being engaged is the student's responsibility. Rather, what teachers do to engage students matters. In my quest to learn as much as I can about student engagement, I discovered that teachers play a major role in cultivating how engaged students are in their learning (Hattie, 2012; Schmoker, 2011). In fact, how engaged a *teacher* is directly relates to how engaged *students* are (Cardwell, 2011).

Teacher perceptions of what defines student engagement have a profound impact on their educational practices (Barkaoui et al., 2015). Essentially, knowing about true engagement will make you a more effective teacher because you will see behaviors in a different way. When you read this book, you will enter the engagement framework and be empowered with information, strategies, and tools. The final chapter pushes teachers and teams to think about the engagement levels that their instructional culture produces and gives you a blueprint to use these concepts to help increase those levels.

No matter what subject or grade level you teach, and no matter how uninterested or directly resistant a student might seem, you can do things tomorrow that will involve students in their learning. I'm going to tell you what those things are. While you may find some of these strategies elsewhere, this book organizes and connects critical, research-based strategies directly to what each of your students need. When you identify students' engagement needs, through either direct observation or data from the student engagement inventories (page 137), you can go directly to the chapter that explains the most critical need and implement the proper strategies.

Every student can engage.

Why Do We Boost Engagement?

While the definition of engagement varies depending on your perspective, engagement is accomplished by connecting with a student's mind and heart. I believe engagement, with its cascade of positive effects that I explain in chapter 1, is the key to increasing learning in your school. This belief comes from my own experience as a student, teacher, parent, and administrator, and it's supported by research.

Let me tell you what's at stake when students don't engage, and what happens when they do.

What's at Stake When Students Don't Engage?

Engagement is a "robust predictor of student learning, grades, achievement, test scores, retention, and graduation" (Skinner & Pitzer, 2012, p. 21). The opposite— when a student is disengaged—is likely to lead to negative feelings about learning, lower achievement, and even dropout (Fredricks, Blumenfeld, & Paris, 2004; Umbach & Wawrzynski, 2005, as cited in Al-Hendawi, 2012). In fact, research tells us that at least 15 percent of students in each United States, Australian, and Canadian school are at the most critical level of disengagement and in danger of dropping out (Guan, 2017; Saeed & Zyngier, 2012; Statistics Canada, 2015).

When students fail and drop out, they are less likely to find jobs, earn living wages, or vote (thus continuing the cycle of low competence and autonomy). They are more likely to be poor and to suffer from a variety of adverse health outcomes (College Board, n.d.; Rumberger, 2011). The Center for Educational Equity's Michael A. Rebell (2017) even warns that the "viability of our democratic institutions is at risk" (p. 3) when students aren't prepared for civic participation.

Academic achievement and positive academic self-concept can help students escape poverty (Jensen, 2019; Stand Together Foundation, 2017) and eventually engage fully as adult citizens, breaking the cycle of disenfranchisement.

Disengagement affects a single person's mental and physical health, but the effects range much further beyond the individual: it has significant economic, social, and global implications.

What Happens When Students Do Engage?

May I tell you a story about the impact of increased engagement in my own classroom? When I began as a middle school teacher at Levey Middle School in Southfield, Michigan, students did not like my class. Levey was a buildingwide Title I school. As a new English teacher, I thought lectures and independent work were what teaching was supposed to look like. I had a bell curve of achievement results. And then my principal, Dr. Anthony Muhammad, challenged me.

Dr. Muhammad saw that I wanted to make a difference but didn't have the tools to do so. As part of every staff meeting, we reviewed articles and books. The staff shared their thoughts, experiences, and feelings. My grade-level team members supported each other with ideas for collaborative work time—community-building experiences for our students. We talked about what strategies worked with our disengaged students. By following through on my team's focus on positive student relationship building and cognitively stimulating, high-interest, multifaceted lessons, I was able to transform my classroom. Dr. Muhammad empowered his teachers with the ability and willingness to try new things and persevere through failure. He helped create a culture of experimentation, and for both teachers and students, thinking of learning as a growth process is beneficial.

In my classes, I had students write, direct, edit, star in, and present short movies to the school community. Like at a film festival, we played the short films over our internal television network. On a Friday afternoon both in the fall and spring, all classes stopped and watched the films our students created. The students loved the project and the learning they did. They were heroes in the hallways. English class became a source of pride for my students, and that fueled intrinsic motivation. The students who watched these student-made movies looked forward to the chance to have their English class create a similar project. It created an atmosphere that celebrated student work. See chapter 5 (page 121) for another example of a film experience we created at Levey.

By the time the state test came around, my students crushed expectations, year in and year out. The success of Levey students was documented by Richard DuFour, Rebecca DuFour, Damen Lopez, and my principal, Anthony Muhammad (2006), in an article titled "Promises Kept":

> The percentage of Levey students meeting standards had more than doubled to 87%, a figure that significantly exceeded the state average for all students and surpassed the state average for black students by 32%. . . . The achievement gap at Levey Middle School has been eliminated. (p. 55)

I share this study because my teaching didn't start this way. I grew with my team as we worked together. It's my wish that you are able to do this, too. I didn't know the research, but I knew that if we could get students to love learning, it would change their lives. I wrote this book to help show you the route. Use what your students find interesting and help transform their school experience to make engagement undeniable.

Improving engagement is worth a school's effort, because when schools focus on that issue, students learn more (Skinner & Pitzer, 2012).

Who Is This Book for?

This book is for all educators, preK to college, including administrators. Instructional leadership demands this knowledge, but the strategies can help at staff meetings, and there is content specific to buildingwide efforts. Many of the concepts, especially those in chapter 1, have informed me as a parent, too. Consider helping your students' parents understand how to help support their children. As it always has been, when learning increases, it changes students' lives for the better. If that is why you're involved in education, we are on the same mission, and you are who this book is for.

K–12 teachers and principals will be able to answer the following questions after reading this book. How do we help students love learning? How do we help students who are already engaged deepen their love for learning? How do we help students who desperately need our assistance getting involved? How does one classroom teacher address years of disengagement and light a fire of passionate learning in students? How can a school or district with a historically underserved population of students transform their classrooms to change lives? Like my story in the beginning of the introduction, think about what you are going to do to help students.

What's in This Book?

The book begins by focusing on the theories for self-efficacy and positive academic self-concept, moves to strategies for addressing different needs, and finishes with a conversation about how to make your classroom culture hospitable to engagement. Note the culture-centric language as you read: *artifacts*, *norms*, and *values* are all present throughout.

Chapter 1 explains two aspects of engagement. The critical nature of developing both aspects—cognitive and affective—are further explained through the filter of a student's academic self-concept (simply, how a student sees his or her academic capabilities). The next two chapters focus on effective strategies that develop cognitive engagement in your classrooms. Chapter 2 shares strategies that help students feel a sense of competence, and chapter 3 shares strategies to develop feelings of autonomy. Chapter 4 shares ways to create positive relationships, or relatedness, with students, while chapter 5 helps make the relevance of classroom content clear to students. Chapter 6 brings the book together, talking about the elements that make up culture and providing an inventory that can reveal students' self-reported engagement levels and help educators make instructional and cultural plans based on their students' needs.

You can read selectively after chapter 1. You don't have to follow a linear order; each chapter stands by itself. Each is structured so that a book study or staff meeting could focus on chapter-specific content and develop rich dialogue about developing academic self-concept. Each chapter begins with a student's school experience. Many of the stories I share are a combination of my experience and my students' experiences; the anecdotes in chapters 2–5 correspond to the concepts of competence, autonomy, relatedness, or relevance. I share multiple researched strategies and, in each case, how to develop those strategies in your classroom or school. The final part of each chapter summarizes that chapter. Strategy-building chapters 2–5 also each have a rubric so you can evaluate how well your classroom facilitates the specific engagement component. As you read through chapters 2–5, think about the norms, values, and beliefs that fill out your classroom's culture.

Some of the information will confirm practices that you already use; other information, I hope, stretches your thinking. Some will require leaving your comfort zone. That's an opportunity to grow. Don't fear failure. It's part of learning! You probably say the same thing to your students. As you read, consider what combination of competence, autonomy, relatedness, and relevance each of your students needs.

CHAPTER 1

THE SELF-EFFICACY CYCLE

Juan looked up at the classroom clock. "Two-thirty already?" He felt cheated that the class was over. "How did time go that fast?" he thought. The eighth grader wanted to keep going.

"I get the biggest kick out of how this class never wants to leave," Mr. Clink said. "Seriously, though, it's time to go home."

Juan was the last student out of the room, and as he left, Mr. Clink said, "Good, hard work today, Juan. You've been making serious jumps. Pretty soon, you're going to be teaching this class."

"I really didn't want to stop today. My story is getting to the best part of my plan. The hero is about to confront the bad guy in an *epic* battle!" Juan had been planning this story, piece by piece, for the better part of two weeks. A classroom anchor chart of that process was hanging on the wall behind Mr. Clink's desk. Juan could see the progress he had made.

"I can't wait to read the story, Juan. Have a great evening. Make sure to study for your other classes too."

Juan shrugged a little. They weren't bad classes, but they weren't like Mr. Clink's.

Both heard the foot traffic in the hallways dwindling. Time before the buses would pull away was getting tight. Mr. Clink held up his fist, knuckles forward for a fist bump. Juan responded in kind and then jogged out of the room to catch his bus.

On the bus, Juan held his paper and a pencil. Juan was going to use his time on the way home to get to the battle scene. As he wrote, he thought, "This is a pretty good story. I'm a pretty good writer. I could be a writer. I could do this," and he continued his masterpiece.

• • • • • • • • • • • • • • • ♥ • • • • • • • • • • • • • • •

As you see in the vignette, Juan was highly engaged in the activity of writing the story. He even seemed to experience *flow* (Csikszentmihalyi, 2008), losing a sense of time due to being so engrossed. His competence was scaffolded at each step with artifacts, and he had visual reminders of his success. He was driven and in control of his story. Finally, he had a connection with the class and with his teacher, who seemed to be on his side. This recipe led to an intrinsically motivated deep learning experience that changed what Juan thought about himself and his ability. The *deep learning* transformed this student's *academic self-concept*, two ideas this chapter elaborates on. In addition to those ideas, this chapter answers these questions with science: What is learning? What is engagement? What is self-determination theory? What is the deep learning cycle of engagement? What is academic self-concept? These questions take you through the self-efficacy cycle.

What Is Learning?

It's important to begin at the basics. What is learning? Is learning simple regurgitation of facts? Is it the skills with which students leave your classroom? According to developmental psychologist Lev S. Vygotsky (1978), learning is a sociocultural activity that occurs when students bridge the gap of inability to ability by crossing the zone of proximal development (as cited in McLeod, 2018). Students come to school with their own understandings, experiences, or skills, and our goal as teachers is to structure interactions that help them through the *zone of proximal development*—the short distance between what students can do and what they need to accomplish (Vygotsky, 1978). As a teacher, you are constantly helping students, each in different ways. Sometimes, it is by what you say, other times it is a classroom strategy you use. Teachers help students enhance skills to the point of independence. You probably remember all of this from your university's introduction to teaching class! Basically, all people can learn, and we help students bridge the gap from dependence to independence.

This zone of proximal development is where competence, autonomy, relatedness, and relevance come in. Pulling students into activities and projects that build these components is how students become independent. When student engagement is transformed and the student's work complexity matches it, students can reach the high-hanging fruit. When complexity and engagement are at their optimal levels, the result is deep learning.

Deep learning, or *deep investigation*, as educators and authors Douglas Fisher, Nancy Frey, and John Hattie (2016) describe it, is where students gain a level of self-regulation and strategic thinking about their learning. You can think of *self-regulation* as a person's ability to manage his or her attention, time, and effort to complete a process. Juan, from the story at the beginning of the chapter, demonstrated self-regulation by getting his story done during class and planning out time to complete it on the bus. Similarly, others describe deep learning as self-regulated, intrinsic motivation (coming from oneself, not external factors), when students feel real interest, enjoyment, and satisfaction with the learning (Ryan & Deci, 2000a, as cited in Saeed & Zyngier, 2012). The metacognitive strategies a learner uses during *deep learning* lead to what all teachers (and students, whether they recognize it or not) seek: the ability for students to successfully demonstrate a transfer of knowledge to the outside world—to become independent (Ford, Smith, Weissbein, Gully, & Salas, 1998). The components examined in this book help build this kind of autonomy and intrinsic motivation.

What Is Engagement?

Academic engagement models are becoming a major focus in preK–12 schools (Al-Hendawi, 2012; Skinner & Pitzer, 2012). What makes one student engage with the learning and another disengage? Different reasons. During a 2018 Michigan Association of State and Federal Program Specialists (MASFPS) conference, I attended a session on student engagement. Participants brainstormed with a poster-making activity. My group had the responsibility of defining engagement. What follows were our responses.

- Active
- Involved
- Actionable
- Interactive
- Articulating the *why*
- Purpose-driven
- Involves voice and choice
- Interested
- Relevant
- Applicable to students' lives
- On the bus
- Purposeful focus

I intentionally did not speak up because I wanted to find out what my colleagues thought. These teachers and principals listed many routines and behaviors for creating engaging instruction or identifying the behavioral norms we would expect to see from engaged students (such as *active*). Basically, we know engagement when we see it, but we might not be so good at understanding how it forms.

How do you think educators should define a student's engagement? This three-part model—(1) cognitive, (2) affective, and (3) behavioral—is an effective construct that many different researchers use (García-Ros, Pérez-González, Tomás, & Fernández, 2017; Green, Nelson, Martin, & Marsh, 2006; Ng, Bartlett, & Elliot, 2018; Orkin, Pott, Wolf, May, & Brand, 2018; Parsons, Nuland, & Parsons, 2014). When a student is engaged, there is a symbiotic growing bond between his or her cognitive (thinking) and affective (feelings) engagement levels (McNeece, 2019). This is an effective model for understanding because it allows us to see that behavior is a byproduct of the cognitive and affective components. The next section goes deeply into each concept.

Engagement Behaviors

The bond between the cognitive and the affective generates engagement behaviors. Figure 1.1 shows the elements that lead to these behaviors and how they connect to self-determination theory (Ryan & Deci, 2009), which I describe later in this chapter (pages 14–17).

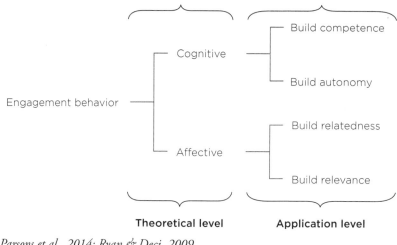

Source: Parsons et al., 2014; Ryan & Deci, 2009.

FIGURE 1.1: Student engagement related to self-determination theory components.

Cognitive

The first component of the model is the cognitive element. Think of it as the intellectual stimulation a student experiences in class. This experience is derived from the organization, structure, and approach—instruction that teachers develop for their students every day. For example, consider the amount of collaborative, or cooperative, learning a teacher has students participate in daily. When students expect a routine of working through daily learning directly with their classmates—bouncing ideas off one another, correcting mistakes, and supporting one another—the learning is deeper (Csikszentmihalyi, 2008). Strategies like this, and the others shared in chapters 2 (page 25) and 3 (page 55), are ways of developing cognitive engagement behaviors.

Students need to be offered new information and have a chance to play with new ideas. Hooking them on a topic occurs when a teacher launches new learning and develops opportunities for students to consolidate their thinking. Consolidation requires academic complexity, interaction, and independence (Fisher & Frey, 2015). This is also the critical time in which a teacher develops a student's sense of competence and autonomy during the learning (Fisher & Frey, 2015; McNeece, 2019).

Affective

Affective engagement is how connected a student feels to the teacher, the other students, and even the content. Teachers see positive or negative affect in the relationships a student has with them, their classmates, and a personal interest with the curriculum. Relationships are critically important to students' academic development. A student's affective connection is also how he or she feels about his or her school leaders and community (Martin & Dowson, 2009). In fact, students who report higher levels of relatedness—a positive affect—with their teachers have higher levels of engagement in their learning (Jamison, 2014).

Affect, like cognition, is something that educators can impact. We can build real relationships with students and cultivate their interest in what they are learning. Relationships are the second key ingredient for engagement. Consider the example at the beginning of this chapter of Juan's positive relationship with his teacher and the story he was writing.

Behavioral

Finally, the behavioral element is the last piece of engagement. Education and human development professors Seth A. Parsons, Leila Richey Nuland, and Allison Ward Parsons (2014) state clearly that the cognitive and affective domains are symbiotic and deeply connected to one another. Their model's behavioral element is a byproduct of students' cognitive and affective connections to a class; students behave in relation to their cognitive and affective connections. A student highly engaged in what he or she is learning and in how he or she is learning it, and one who is feeling connected to the classroom, translates this engagement to on-task behaviors like paying attention, working hard, participating in class, and resilience (Hart, Stewart, & Jimerson, 2011). It's these behaviors that some educators misunderstand as engagement, when in fact they are the result of it.

Have you ever noticed how the same teachers have great classes year after year? This is not coincidental, and it's not the luck of the draw. These teachers actively cultivate their strategies and behaviors. Also, have you noticed a student putting more effort into her work after the two of you have developed a positive relationship? After discipline, does a student's effort suffer? Our experiences as teachers usually align with the research that says when a student has trouble in either the cognitive or affective element, they are likely to develop a problem with the other (Cairns & Cairns, 1994; Estell, Farmer, & Cairns, 2007, as cited in Farmer et al., 2011).

Four Types of Classroom Engagement Cultures

The cognitive and affective elements intersect, creating a matrix of four classroom engagement cultures.

1. Low cognitive, low affective
2. High cognitive, high affective
3. Low cognitive, high affective
4. High cognitive, low affective

Seeing these cultures can help teachers reflect on their practices. Figure 1.2 plots the four engagement classroom types.

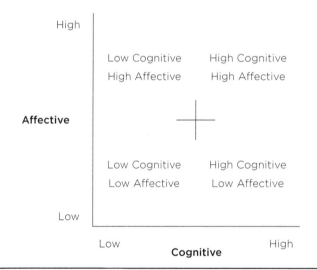

FIGURE 1.2: Classroom culture types.

High cognitive, high affective is full engagement. Students feel like they belong and are respected. The students are pushed academically and cared for personally. They deepen their understanding and have positive academic self-concepts.

Low cognitive, high affective classrooms are where the teacher is the buddy, but the level of deep learning is low. These students will enjoy class due to the relationships and may even report positive feelings about school but will not gain positive academic self-concepts. These students are at risk for falling behind academically due to the lack of deep learning. Given that Fisher et al. (2016) report that 90 percent of all classroom learning is only surface level, low cognitive engagement is the norm in many schools.

High cognitive, low affective classrooms have teachers who believe rigor is the purest determiner of success. The students who make it through this class's mine-fields will have positive academic self-concepts, but the overall results will be mixed. Students who need to feel connected to the teacher or the curriculum will not fully realize their potential in this classroom.

Low cognitive, low affective classrooms are dangerous places for students. They are not being academically challenged nor are they feeling connection. These classrooms disengage students from their learning and have lasting effects on their education long after they leave that particular class (Mangiante, 2011; Muhammad, 2009, 2018). This can occur because a student has a teacher who shows he or she cares for students neither personally or academically. These students have negative academic self-concepts.

Monotonous sit-and-get lessons don't change lives, and they *do* create the opportunity for students to fall away from learning. Professor Elaine M. Silva Mangiante (2011) cites William L. Sanders and June C. Rivers (1996) when she says:

> Students assigned to ineffective teachers over the course of several years demonstrate significantly lower academic achievement than those students who are assigned to several highly effective teachers in a row indicating that teacher effects on students are both additive and cumulative. (p. 42)

Think about each of these four classrooms' cultures. How will artifacts, values, and beliefs—the ways culture shows itself in a classroom—look in each of them (Schein, 2010)? What would you expect to see if you walked into a high cognitive, high affective classroom? What about a low cognitive, low affective classroom? Do you see classroom instruction in your school that reflects any or all of these types? Did inexperienced teaching result in low cognitive, high affective culture, and has experience gotten your class culture closer to high cognitive, high affective? (Chapter 6, page 129, explains the definition and components of a classroom engagement culture. Teachers are classroom leaders. This role should not be undervalued, and everyone should know the positive results.)

Understanding engagement through this filter enables educators to further understand what we can do to help our students become more engaged. The last piece of the engagement puzzle is the component of the self-determination theory (Ryan & Deci, 2009) and how that blends with the three-part model described so far (García-Ros et al., 2017; Green et al., 2006; Ng et al., 2018; Orkin et al., 2018; Parsons et al., 2014).

What Is Self-Determination Theory?

Understanding how to create an engaging classroom requires breaking down the cognitive and affective pieces one level further. As we saw, the behavioral engagement that students demonstrate is a manifestation of the cognitive and affective elements. Psychology professors Richard M. Ryan and Edward L. Deci's (2000b) self-determination theory (SDT) also allows us to *quantify* and increase student engagement, as you will see in chapter 6.

SDT is about motivation. It suggests that people are motivated in many ways, some by external influences (Ryan & Deci, 2000a, 2000b). Other people base their decisions and behaviors on their own goals (Martin, 2012). The latter is called *intrinsic motivation* because it comes from inside a person. It is not triggered by a controlled prompt (Martin, 2012). Have you ever participated in a committee—something you weren't passionate about—because your boss asked you to? Did you have household chores when you were younger because your parents required it? The motivators for these activities are extrinsic.

On the other hand, have you ever been a part of a team or organization that was a personal passion? When we make choices based on intrinsic motivation, we find enjoyment or satisfaction when we participate. This motivation is more powerful than extrinsic. When looking at a classroom, instead of students complying with academic behaviors because of their motivation to earn good grades or recognition for high achievement, the ideal is for students to learn because they are compelled by the content and eager to know more.

Where does that intrinsic motivation get its start? Deci and Ryan (2000a, 2000b) find that it builds when we achieve three things: (1) competence, (2) autonomy, and (3) relatedness. Self-determination theory and academic self-concept are connected through those elements and through the very important final element, relevance to content, which is a form of relatedness. Look back at figure 1.1 (page 10) again to see this connection illustrated.

The cycle begins to form here, since students with positive academic self-concepts (see pages 19–21) have strong and statistically significant levels of intrinsic motivation (Lohbeck, 2016). According to the same research, students become less motivated and even amotivated when they report lower levels of academic self-concept (Lohbeck, 2016). *Amotivated* students focus on disrupting and usurping the learning in class (Appleton, Christenson, & Furlong, 2008; McNeece, 2019).

Unmotivated and amotivated students feel detached from their classes and show it by sleeping in, skipping, or interrupting class. Have you experienced a student in full rebellion? Someone who, if you say *up*, says *down*? Developing positive academic self-concept is the key to helping those students choose behaviors that are not self-sabotaging (Lohbeck, 2016).

Competence, autonomy, and relatedness are explained in the following sections.

Competence

Feelings of competence are the first level of cognitive engagement. As explained in Ryan and Deci's (2000b) SDT, *competence* is how someone perceives his or her skills and abilities to eventually meet a goal. When I think that I'm good at something, I feel competent.

Here's how competence relates to engagement: research shows that a student's belief in his or her academic competence strongly correlates with how engaged he or she is (Jackson, 2011; Legault, Green-Demers, & Pelletier, 2006). If students don't feel competent, they may avoid tasks—even those they are capable of accomplishing (Deed, 2008). Feeling competent is also connected to mastery orientation.

You can help students develop a sense of competence by doing the following, which are discussed in depth in chapter 2 (page 25).

- Promoting mastery orientation (Jackson, 2011)
- Providing formative feedback (Marzano, 2007)
- Using cooperative learning (Fisher, Frey, & Lapp, 2011; McNeece, 2019)
- Encouraging reflection (Desautel, 2009)

Chapter 2 expands the ideas and modes in the preceding list into specific strategies.

Autonomy

Autonomy is the second element of cognitive engagement. *Autonomy* is freedom, control, and the liberty to set and meet goals. Our minds seek autonomy (Deci & Ryan, 2014). Increased control by developing student voice and employing democracy where possible results in more effective teaching (Muhammad & Hollie, 2012; Orkin et al., 2018).

Building autonomy into a classroom is critical. A lack of control over learning means students are usually unsure how to do well. Feeling like we have minimal control strongly correlates with anxiety (Martin, 2003). Younger students seek to feel older and more in control, and I probably do not have to tell you how teenagers respond to a lack of control.

You can provide structured autonomy. Help disengaged students develop the meta-cognitive strategies that help them become aware of their own thinking (McNeece, 2019). During guided instruction, model how the students use metacognitive questions or get through the hardest part of a lesson. During cooperative learning (which is sometimes referred to as *collaborative learning*), students practice these skills when they ask or answer questions. As you can guess, students who perceive greater classroom-based autonomy have greater interest, engagement, and performance (Reeve & Jang, 2006).

Teachers who encourage student autonomy do the following (Orkin et al., 2018), which are discussed in depth in chapter 3 (page 55).

- Support students' deciding how they want to practice with concepts.
- Allow multiple paths to learning target demonstration.
- Use cooperative learning strategies (like those in chapter 2 and chapter 3) that specifically focus on building autonomy.
- Share decision-making power.

Relatedness

Students' relationships with their teachers have the greatest impact on student learning and are critical for the most disengaged students (McNeece, 2019). SDT's *relatedness* and *affective engagement* are practically the same thing. Relatedness levels are based on how connected a student feels to the teacher and classmates. Each component impacts the other. Teacher relatedness has a significant relationship to engagement and achievement (Rolland, 2012). More interestingly, when students report higher levels of relatedness to their teachers, they are more likely to report a greater sense of peer-to-peer relatedness and higher engagement (Furrer & Skinner, 2003).

Did you have a good relationship with any of your teachers? If so, how did it change your perspective of the class? Did you connect with your classmates, and did that make it easier for you to participate? Students "need frequent, affective pleasant or positive interactions with the same individuals, and they need these interactions to occur in a framework of long-term, stable caring, and concern" (Baumeister & Leary, 1995, p. 520). More emotional support from teachers develops students who have more cognitive, emotional, and social engagement (Rimm-Kaufman, Baroody, Larsen, Curby, & Abry, 2015). Harvard professor Ronald F. Ferguson and colleagues (2015) state that a caring teacher is a necessity for all students learning at high levels. Australian researcher John Hattie (2012) in *Visible Learning for Teachers* ranks student-teacher relationships among the most powerful educational components to have an impact on student learning. The abundance of research confirming this impact is clear.

And learning is a social process (Vygotsky, 1978). Do the students in your classroom help one another? How can you help foster your students' connections to one another and to school as a whole?

Educators devoted to developing relatedness will do the following, and chapter 4 (page 79) discusses these in detail.

- Develop supportive, caring, and collaborative structures both among the students and between the student and the teacher (Furrer & Skinner, 2003).
- Build students' connections to their classmates and the school (Furrer & Skinner, 2003).
- Monitor their own personal biases (McNeece, 2019).

Relevance

Finally, students also need to have an affective connection to what they are learning. Relatedness to content—*relevance*—is also part of intrinsic motivation. Interest in a topic helps a student engage, and it is also critical for students to hear the value of what they are learning and the relationship it has to their lives and aspirations (Corso, Bundick, Quaglia, & Haywood, 2013; Orkin et al., 2018). In my experience, this element is the most neglected.

Do you know your students and their interests? Do you weave their world and youth culture into content? Have you ever taken a previous year's lesson and changed your method of delivery to help students experience something different? Have you structured a lesson to launch it differently?

Educators devoted to developing relevance will do the following, and chapter 5 (page 107) discusses these in detail.

- Work to understand students' interests and integrate them into daily aspects.
- Use interesting demonstrations and explanations when delivering content and model learning.
- Support student growth beyond the classroom and beyond the typical scope of learning.

What Is the Deep Learning Cycle of Engagement?

Students who develop a love for learning—an intrinsic drive—produce and strengthen the strategies that allow their learning to transfer to life. Think about your own life and your passions. One of my passions is writing, and, as you learned at the beginning of the book, it was not always that way. Today, I lose myself and sense of time when I sit to write. As I have begun to see myself more and more as a writer, I go deeper in my thinking to adjust the messages to help my readers incrementally develop their thinking toward the end goal—the *what*, the *how* and, most importantly, the *why*. This *deep learning* is fostered when a teacher has developed a cognitive and affective environment and grows, supports, and enhances student competence, autonomy, relatedness, and relevance. Deep learning is the result of highly complex tasks coupled with high engagement; think of this as when a student has found his or her mission (McNeece, 2019). Just as Juan didn't want to stop working, deep learning will be the experience of students in classrooms that create an environment such as the one in the introduction.

What is deep learning? Fisher et al. (2016) explain that the students who are doing it "interact with the content and ideas, and actively link concepts and knowledge across content" (p. 73). This is opposed to students who stay on the surface of learning and depend on activities like memorization (Fisher et al., 2016). Deep learners set personal goals and check to ensure their understanding (Dean, Hubbell, Pitler, & Stone, 2012). Neuroscience seems to confirm how and why this cycle creates deeper learning. Cognitive and affective connections stimulate the production of feel-good chemicals dopamine and oxytocin, while decreasing catecholamines, a stress-response chemical (Jackson, 2011). This mix of chemicals increases creativity and persistence and stimulates the brain's dendrites to make stronger connections, increasing ability (Jackson, 2011; Tate, 2010).

The outcomes from deep learning create a cycle of engagement that accelerates the student to a higher level of thinking (Buckner et al., 2016). Given this is a cycle, each dive into the learning is like a shovel digging a hole in a garden. It gets deeper and wider each push. Each time a student deeply learns, he or she develops and reinforces the behaviors that create success. The student builds on prior successes and knowledge to scaffold new learning. From my experience in the classroom, this makes practice and comprehension more efficient as well. It is akin to when a student reads more and hence becomes a better reader.

Consistent with neuroscience, these engaged students report higher-level thinking and greater metacognitive strategies than their peers (McInerney, Cheng, Mok, &

Lam, 2012). They use analysis, synthesis, judgment, and theory application to independently develop greater understanding. Deep learning also results in students creating strategies and applying the new learning (McInerney et al., 2012). Finally, Fisher et al. (2016) share that deep learning generates the ability to transfer what someone has learned in the classroom to the real world—teaching's main purpose, I would argue.

What Is Academic Self-Concept?

For all students, academic self-concept, intrinsic motivation, and academic outcomes are all connected (Martin, 2012). Everyone has what psychologists describe as a *self-concept*. It is who you think you are. *Academic self-concept* is nearly the same, but in the realm of learning. It is how students "perceive their strengths, weaknesses, abilities, attitudes, and values" (McInerney et al., 2012, p. 250).

Our perceptions of our abilities—I am good at this, but I really stink at that—become our realities; therefore, developing positive academic self-concepts is a key to closing the achievement gap *and* the engagement gap. You have probably worked with students who feel they are not good at school. How do you think that notion developed? Consider the most dramatic intervention schools use when a student significantly struggles—retention. Students who have been retained in a grade feel a very negative impact on their academic self-concepts. Not only that, Hattie's (2012) research finds that retention has a strong negative impact on a student's actual learning. These students have been formally told by their schools they are not capable of moving on with their friends and peers.

One of my favorite teachers, Christie Bronson, was teaching kindergarten when I became a principal. Christie had been in the classroom teaching for over forty years when I started. She was teaching the grandkids of former students! Christie was against retention and explained why. As a kindergarten teacher, she met with all the parents and students before the year started. Christie says that in her experience, if one of the parents had been retained as a student, fear that the same could happen to his or her child was the first thing the parent would share with her. They were afraid their children would be retained before the children had experienced even a single day of school. Even twenty or thirty years after feeling like an academic failure, the experience of visible failure still heavily influences a parent's perceptions of school and his or her own child's experience. Retention had done permanent damage to the parent's academic self-concept.

Academic self-concept exists on a continuum, as shown in figure 1.3 (page 20).

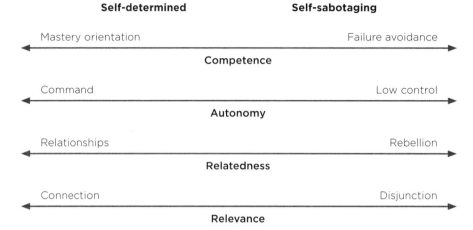

Source: Adapted from Martin, 2003, 2007; Martin & Dowson, 2009; Ryan & Deci, 2000a.

FIGURE 1.3: Academic self-concept continuum.

Self-sabotaging students are thought to exhibit defense mechanisms like failure avoidance to protect their self-esteem (Buckner et al., 2016). Self-sabotage plays a significant role in student underperformance (Schwinger, Wirthwein, Lemmer, & Steinmayr, 2014, as cited in Buckner et al., 2016). How would you characterize your students' self-concepts? Have you ever seen a student sabotage him- or herself? Has a student come to you missing skills or shut down to new learning? How did you change that student's school experience? Were you able to increase his or her intrinsic motivation? How?

Akin to deep learning, students form academic self-concept through their school environments (Shavelson, Hubner, & Stanton, 1976, as cited in Green et al., 2006). The cognitive and affective engagement developed in school by both teachers and administrators are what lead to the formation of academic self-concept.

In the following points, look at academic self-concept through the competence, autonomy, relatedness, and relevance filters to turn theory into classroom action.

- Competence is where students see work and challenge as capacity-building toward mastery orientation (Haimovitz & Dweck, 2017). Failure avoidance, which can result from lack of feeling competent, is an effort to avoid risk or embarrassment (Haimovitz & Dweck, 2017; Snipes & Tran, 2017). See chapter 2 (page 25).

- Exercising autonomy gives students command over their learning and allows them to see the progression so they can accomplish tasks. Having low or no control is motivationally draining because the student can't see where to put his or her energy to grow (Martin, 2007). See chapter 3 (page 55).

- Fostering positive, warm relationships with the teacher helps students move away from disaffection and rebellion, so they can focus on learning (Furrer, Skinner, & Pitzer, 2014). See chapter 4 (page 79).

- Seeing how what they are learning relates to their lives connects students to the content (Green et al., 2006). Sparking their interests moves their perspectives beyond the classroom (Schilling, 2009). See chapter 5 (page 107).

Students with positive academic self-concepts learn more than their peers (Dweck, 2006; Green et al., 2006; Hattie, 2012; Marzano, 2007), perhaps because academic self-concept and motivation are interwoven (Ahmed & Bruinsma, 2006; Green et al., 2006). You probably have experienced this in your classroom. Higher achievement and academic self-concept have a reciprocal relationship. Students who are confident about their academic abilities outperform their classmates. Positive academic self-concept can result in increased achievement by students from lower socioeconomic statuses, less supportive backgrounds, and low prior achievement (Guay, Larose, & Boivin, 2004; Marsh, 1991; Marsh & Yeung, 1997; Parker et al., 2012, as cited in Seaton, Parker, Marsh, Craven, & Yeung, 2014). This is significant research because a teacher, knowledgeable and able to implement the proper strategies to build academic self-concept, will change the lives of struggling students.

Luckily, as teachers we create the cultures that engage and support students in ways that lead to positive academic self-concept (Shavelson et al., 1976, as cited in Green et al., 2006). When students grow to believe in their abilities, feel they have control over their learning, and have solid relationships with the teachers and their classmates, the result is engagement and positive academic self-concept. Teachers affect all of this.

With a positive academic self-concept, the student also develops (and the teacher helps create) more self-efficacy (Ferla, Valcke, & Cai, 2009), which makes students feel in command of their learning.

What Is the Self-Efficacy Cycle?

Self-efficacy is the sense that through our own activity, we make learning happen. Research in classrooms shows that self-efficacy has a dramatic impact on student learning (Hattie, 2012). Have you personally experienced a sense of self-efficacy after puzzling through a difficult problem and developing a way to solve it? You probably felt especially capable. We do this all the time as teachers. We take experiences from past successes, reflect on where a student's problems are, and formulate a plan for his or her success. Figuring out how to help students could be the puzzle that helps teachers *themselves* develop self-efficacy while also helping students. Teachers use deep learning all the time to help struggling learners, and the information in the following chapters is part of your deep investigation of teaching.

Self-efficacy leads to higher educational outcomes and a better academic self-concept which supports even higher levels of engagement (figure 1.4). It is called the *self-efficacy cycle* because each component—engagement, self-concept, learning, and so on—strengthens another.

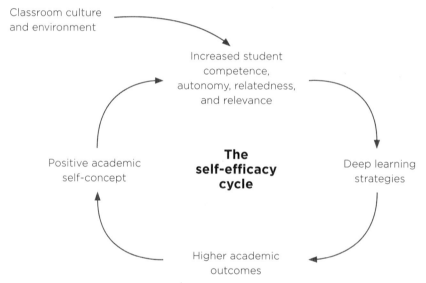

Source: Adapted from Buckner et al., 2016, Csikszentmihalyi, 1991; Fisher et al., 2016; Hattie, 2012; Marzano, 2007; Reeve, 2012; Rolland, 2012; Snipes & Tran, 2017.

FIGURE 1.4: The self-efficacy cycle.

Believing in oneself is very important, but the self-efficacy cycle describes the *process* of empowering learners and helping transform a student's thinking, abilities, and behaviors. Therefore, self-belief alone is not enough to maintain or even begin this cycle. The student must also have the cognitive environment, developed by the teacher, to truly reach deep learning and continue through the cycle.

This sounds simple: we reproduce a behavior when we receive positive reinforcement—but it is more complicated than that. It may seem like common sense, but remember that the cycle encompasses all of what appears in figure 1.1 (page 10)—

all the engagement components of the theoretical level (cognitive, affective, and behavioral), the application level (competence, autonomy, relatedness, and relevance), and deep learning. Students' academic self-concepts—perceptions of one's own abilities (strengths, weaknesses, abilities, attitudes, and values)—are a direct result of a classroom's culture.

In a way of thinking, *academic self-concept* is the noun and *self-efficacy* is the verb. *Academic self-concept* is the title, and *self-efficacy* is the action. Even though they are considered separate theories, when students are asked what their academic self-concepts are, their responses correlate to their self-efficacy skill levels (Ferla et al., 2009). Students do not have high self-efficacy in school when they have negative academic self-concepts. Positive academic self-concept is the final piece of the self-efficacy cycle, and it helps students through rigorous learning.

Students with high self-efficacy do the following.

- See complex tasks as challenges to master.
- Think of failure as a chance to learn, and understand they need more time, effort, information, or support.
- Recover from losses or setbacks (Fisher et al., 2016).
- Increase levels of persistence (Green et al., 2006; Martin, 2003).

Students with lower self-efficacy do the following.

- Demonstrate failure avoidance in the classroom.
- Have low commitment to goals.
- Think of failure as a lack of ability or intelligence.
- Are slow to recover from losses or setbacks (Fisher et al., 2016).

To help you determine what your students need, the appendix (page 137) contains an adapted diagnostic so you and your colleagues can quickly gather engagement data from students. These data allow you to plan self-efficacious behavior building and help your students develop positive academic self-concepts.

Summary

The psychological research and framework that this book uses are scaffolding to help you evaluate and build your classroom's culture of engagement. It is critically important to know what engagement *really* is and how to develop it in students. If we can build self-efficacy behaviors in your students, we can change their lives.

I developed the engagement evaluation tool and the remaining chapters to help you develop the academic self-concept of your most unmotivated or disengaged students. If they can't love what they learn, they will always have a negative academic self-concept.

Remember the student, Juan, at the beginning of the chapter? He was developing a positive academic self-concept because of his classroom's culture. This is what I want, and what you want, for all your students.

CHAPTER 2

COMPETENCE

Rachel looked around at her group—five different students from her third grade. They were all looking through the two-page story and answering questions the teacher had put on the board.

A girl from the group was trying to answer one particular question and tentatively said, "I think the character is happy about the family's visit to the zoo." The boy next to her spoke up, asking "What in the story tells us that?" His eyes scanned the front page of the story.

Weeks before, Rachel would have never spoken up in this group, but she liked working with her peers now. Last year, she disliked the reading part of her day, but her feelings had changed this year. She shared something now in response to the boy's question: "On the second page, the girl in the story mentions how much fun she had on the zoo's carousel." The teacher was passing by as the group collaborated, and she stopped when she heard the comment.

"Rachel, I think you're on to something there. You've got this. What specifically does the character say?" Mrs. Kay intentionally pushed Rachel's thinking with the comment. Rachel went back to the passage, reread, found what she thought might be the answer, touched the page with her finger, and shared it with the group. The other members nodded.

"That's good thinking, and your effort to search all through the story was very helpful. Where else in the story can you find evidence?" Mrs. Kay said as she smiled, giving the team a thumbs-up and moving on. Rachel peeked up at the wall where the unit steps were displayed. They were halfway through, and today was about finding the answers in the story. She felt confident about her skills.

"Good. Rachel found the first piece of evidence. We just need one more," one of the team members said. The students smiled and turned their attention back to the story.

Rachel thought about it being a tough assignment, but giving up didn't even cross her mind. She knew she could get it done and was not afraid of working to do it. "I'm pretty good at reading," she thought to herself.

• • • • • • • • • • • • • • • ♥ • • • • • • • • • • • • • • •

Rachel's experiences in Mrs. Kay's reading block helped her develop a sense of competence, leading to a stronger academic self-concept. Her teacher helped the team understand that it was possible to find the information they were looking for. She also affirmed the work they had done while making it clear that they had only found part of the evidence so far. Rachel persisted and did not step back from the rigors of the task.

Rachel's competence included many elements, which I discuss in this chapter, and Mrs. Kay could continue fostering that with a number of competence-building strategies like those I include here. As you read the chapter, think about your classroom culture of competence building, and at the end, use the "Teacher Self-Assessment Rubric—Competence" reproducible (pages 53–54) to evaluate it.

We can break down the elements of competence into competence-building strategies that lead you and your students to this kind of engagement.

Elements of Competence

Not a person reading this book can say he or she has not learned from a mistake. As educators, we understand that learning is a process. Some students do not see learning this way. Instead, they want the correct answer or the perfect score. They do not necessarily see the effort as valuable or see mistakes as important to their growth. How did they come to this perspective? There are probably many answers to the question, but most of the responsibility falls on the traditional educational system, which focuses on the task score instead of the learning process. Luckily, this is something that we can change.

I have the great fortune of being married to an artist. I always assumed that some people can draw, paint, or sculpt, and that others cannot. I also thought that artists have the perfect images in their minds before beginning their work. This may be true on some level for some artists, but the act of applying thought and emotion to materials is a process that requires a great deal of trial and error. Artists have to adjust to human errors as a piece develops. They incorporate mistakes into the artwork so in the end, the mistake is not an error but an integral part of the piece. Think of Michelangelo's sculpture of David. The marble from which he was carved was deeply flawed, and rejected by all other master artists of that time (Encyclopedia Britannica, n.d.). Michelangelo chose the marble and used the flaws to develop a masterpiece.

The work someone puts in helps develop his or her ability—competence. On the continuum in figure 1.3 (page 20), the positive side of competence is mastery orientation. In the vignette at the beginning of the chapter, Rachel was working hard to find the answers. She was demonstrating mastery orientation.

Teachers can contribute to some elements of competence, including growth mindset, formative assessment, and reflection. A classroom that builds a mastery orientation does the following very specific things, explained in this chapter.

- Helps students understand challenges as a method to improve ability and increase persistence (in other words, *develop a growth mindset*; Dweck, 2006; Jackson, 2011)

- Provides feedback (Marzano, 2007)

- Includes a structured platform or ability tree exhibiting student growth (Orkin et al., 2018)

- Uses cooperative learning to scaffold confidence (Fisher et al., 2011; McNeece, 2019)

- Uses reflection strategies (Desautel, 2009)

Growth Mindset

Mastery orientation describes a student who works to *develop* competence instead of working to *demonstrate* competence (Rolland, 2012). The difference may seem small, but it is large. Students who work to *develop* mastery are seeking to improve, and students who want to *demonstrate* mastery are looking for a grade—an extrinsic motivator. The most intrinsically motivated students will be those who love to learn and who are diving deeper into an area of study (McNeece, 2019). They have what Carol S. Dweck (2006) calls a *growth mindset*. They believe in intelligence's malleability. Growth mindset thinkers feel their intelligence grow as they struggle, work hard, and even fail; they also have higher academic outcomes due to producing deeper learning strategies (Snipes & Tran, 2017). Dweck (2015) confirms that students "need to try new strategies and seek input from others when they're stuck. They need this repertoire of approaches—not just sheer effort—to learn and improve."

Mastery orientation and growth mindset empower students with self-determining skills like perseverance (Snipes & Tran, 2017) and persistence (Green et al., 2006; Martin, 2003). Think of all the state and college entrance exams that students must take over their educational careers. These tests are long and challenging. Students with strong self-concepts of competence have staying power on these tests. More importantly, think of all the deep learning that a persistent student can accomplish on a long-term project. Students with a mastery orientation develop distinct behaviors that allow them to succeed. They set goals, show tremendous effort, react well to setbacks, and bounce back faster after failure (Haimovitz & Dweck, 2017).

Failure avoidance is the other side of the academic self-concept competence continuum. *Failure avoidance* is what a student is doing when he or she is reluctant to even try due to the fear of possible failure; it inhibits academic school success (Farrington et al., 2012). Students with this behavior view failure as a loss or a sign of stupidity (Dweck, 2006) and that begets a fear of even trying. In juxtaposition to the students with a mastery orientation, students with lower competence do not view failure as an opportunity to learn from a mistake; it reaffirms their worldview that they are not good at whatever they're attempting.

You witness failure avoidance at nearly every sporting event. Look at the players when a lopsided game or match is coming to an end. Many times, the players' heads are down and their intensity tapers off. A championship team, even when losing, never thinks they are out of the game. The intensity doesn't waiver. More to the point, teams that view losses as a pathway to analyzing their plays are far more suited for future victories than a team that sees losing as a mark of their ability. In my coaching experience, teams that focus on wins and losses can sabotage the season by missing practices, working lackadaisically, and blaming teammates after a loss.

Students who are self-sabotaging do the same thing when they think learning is out of reach. Students who report lower self-efficacy behaviors also report higher levels of failure avoidance in class (Snipes & Tran, 2017). Self-sabotaging students have significantly more performance avoidance (Buckner et al., 2016) and are even afraid of attempting things over concerns of potential embarrassment or being seen as failures (Snipes & Tran, 2017). Structuring your classroom environment to help develop a mastery orientation can benefit every student in the classroom (Haimovitz & Dweck, 2017).

How are your students' academic self-concepts in terms of competence? How can you help them grow and change their levels of competence? A classroom that builds this element in its students does very specific things, and this chapter explains those.

Now, let's switch our focus to the research-based strategies that will help your students build a sense of competence in your classroom: formative assessment and reflection.

Formative Assessment

Formative assessment is different than a final test or summative assessment. *Formative assessment* essentially means any assessment where the data adjust instruction, and *common* formative assessments—those built and implemented across grades or subjects per a PLC—allow teacher teams to "share instructional strategies" and effectively use data to determine which strategies are working (Bailey & Jakicic, 2012, p. 17). Think of it as a chef taste-testing a sauce so he or she knows what ingredient to add. Formative assessment increases self-efficacy, producing many of the positive behaviors discussed in chapter 1 (page 7; Bailey & Heritage, 2018).

When you use formative assessment and give feedback, how does this transform a student's sense of competence? Overall, the feedback must communicate the teacher's belief that the student is on the path to get it. Students need to know that it is possible to produce high-quality work if they continue (Snipes & Tran, 2017). When a teacher does accurately communicate this, it increases the quality of student work (Yeager et al., 2014). Feedback on prior performance increases a student's self-efficacy the next time he or she takes on that task (Anseel, Lievens, & Schollaert, 2009, as cited in Di Stefano, Gino, Pisano, & Staats, 2016). This is consistent with the self-efficacy cycle (figure 1.4, page 22).

You don't need a game or ice breaker to gather information and help a student grow competence. Asking your students questions and giving them meaningful feedback are just as effective. How's it going? Do you have questions about any part of what you're working on? Where are you planning to begin?

SCHOOLWIDE COMPETENCE SUPPORT

To help support schoolwide competence building, consider using this chapter's strategies as support in all classrooms. For example, if your building chooses to use formative assessment as that buildingwide initiative, make sure you support that effort.

- Use staff meeting time to introduce, discuss, or reintroduce the concept. Use this chapter as a jumping-off point, but also tap into the expertise in the room. There are probably teachers in your building who are using formative assessment strategies. Use prompting questions to discover and highlight those. Allow the teachers in your building to demonstrate leadership in these critical competence-building areas.

- Everyone should use it, including the principal, if it's for everyone in every classroom. Make sure you, the building's instructional leader, use formative assessment during your staff meetings. In my experience, when leaders step out of their comfort zone and try to model these behaviors, staff are more willing to go further while using those strategies in the classroom.

- Include *instructional rounds* with your chosen strategy, where groups of teachers observe other teachers' practices and have time to talk and reflect (City, Elmore, Fiarman, & Teitel, 2009). See chapter 5 (page 107) for a detailed description.

Reflection

Stimulating reflection and honest self-assessment are key, for any lesson, to helping students develop deep learning (Young, 2018) and positive academic self-concepts. Being able to reflect and self-assess increases self-efficacy, which allows students to see how far they have come (Di Stefano et al., 2016). It is a way they can acknowledge their own growth and see what behaviors helped them succeed. John Dewey (1933), grandfather of education reform, states that we do not learn from experience but, instead, we learn from reflection on experience.

I reflect when coaching younger athletes. Once, my team was behind in a championship game. At halftime, I began by reminding them of the first day of practice, when many of them couldn't complete a challenging relay. I talked about how those failures made them stronger. I provoked their reflection so they could think about how much they had developed. During the second half, we came back and won the game in much the same way they had developed through the season, one play at a time.

Coaching and teaching are very much the same thing. This process is one part of making sense of the information and one part thinking about *how* they learned, or *metacognition* (Davis, 2003). When reflections, such as goal setting related to an ability tree (pages 41–45), occur routinely and collaboratively, the results lead to powerful growth of student competence (Desautel, 2009).

Competence-Building Strategies

These are not the only strategies for building competence, but those I have included here are what research identifies as the most *effective*. With small adaptations, you can use these growth mindset, formative assessment, and reflection strategies in any classroom, from preK to college.

Growth Mindset Strategies

Students with growth mindsets believe they can develop their intelligence through hard work, good thinking strategies (that teachers model), and instruction (Blackwell, Trzesniewski, & Dweck, 2007; Dweck & Leggett, 1988, as cited in Haimovitz & Dweck, 2017). Consider how you might weave Dweck's (2006) theory into your classroom, because it will help you build your students' levels of mastery orientation. In Hattie's (2017) updated list of effective strategies, *conceptual change programs* (teaching methods that give students new mental models to see the world) have a very strong affect—over double the educational impact of a normal year in school. Talking about growth mindset with your students, revealing the misconceptions that come with a fixed mindset, is an excellent way to grow a student's sense of competence.

Many schools are doing this. It is hard to miss the posters and language that many classrooms are using about building growth mindsets. It is important to understand that a poster on the wall that says "Failure is the first step to success" is not enough. Teachers, personally, tend to report very high levels of growth-minded thinking; although the students of those teachers don't respond with the same levels of growth mindset (Haimovitz & Dweck, 2017; Snipes & Tran, 2017). Sadly, our thinking about how we can develop intelligence doesn't translate to our students without some intentional processes (Haimovitz & Dweck, 2017; Young, 2018). Growth requires a sustained focus and examples from both students' and the teacher's experiences. Regularly point out a student's increased level of competence connected with the learning process; call to mind failures that occurred along the way to that success. The theory requires deeper classroom culture change and intentional communication to lead to growth in students.

The first step is to develop a growth mindset as an intervention for your students. There is a growing body of evidence about the fruitfulness of developing interventions that focus on building students' growth mindsets (Snipes & Tran, 2017). This process to build a growth mindset intervention will look different at every school and every grade level, but research tells us there are required consistencies. The following necessary consistencies are adapted from three sources (Blackwell et al., 2007; Good, Aronson, & Inzlicht, 2003, as cited in Snipes & Tran, 2017; Haimovitz & Dweck, 2017). The studies that use the following growth mindset intervention methods find increased academic performance (Snipes & Tran, 2017).

- Distinguishing between growth and fixed mindsets
- Using praise properly
- Communicating with parents and guardians to help them also build a growth mindset in their children
- Giving feedback that deepens understandings, shows incremental growth, and harnesses the power of *yet* (Haimovitz & Dweck, 2017)

The following sections examine each of these methods in detail.

Growth Versus Fixed Mindset Differentiation

Help students learn what a growth mindset is and compare it to a fixed mindset. A growth mindset is explained on page 27. A *fixed mindset* is when someone believes that intelligence is fixed and something that cannot be improved (Dweck, 2006). A student with a fixed mindset will demonstrate task avoidance when he or she believes success isn't possible.

Making the concepts of a growth mindset clear during class time is important. Luckily, there are easy ways to communicate these concepts to your students (Haimovitz & Dweck, 2017).

- Try using analogies. Ask, "Did you ever see a baby learn to walk? Did it happen in a day? Did the baby go from sitting to sprinting in a day?"

- Share concepts through individual mentoring, small group, or whole-class format. Additional classroom resources for students to see and hear are crucial. Think of picking out a class novel for a growth mindset character arc or putting together a bulletin board in a mathematics class that highlights a common mistake students made on a test and how the class has learned to solve the problem properly.

- Have a growth mindset show-and-tell for a few minutes in the beginning or end of the day or class. Give students a chance to say how a growth mindset helps them in or out of school. After a teacher models how to do this, students sharing life experiences is an excellent way to help students understand why *not* having a fixed mindset is so important.

- Consider doing something formal, like a research project on fixed and growth mindsets. During the activity, students discuss and create a presentation or final poster to display in the room. Do this activity multiple times through the year. Have students interview parents and community members, and perhaps have students use their own growth mindset experiences as part of the research.

- Model a growth mindset during class with think-alouds. They let students see inside your head, glimpsing perseverance and what it looks like. Simply say what you're thinking (or what your students might be thinking) as you solve a problem or approach a revision.

- Acknowledge that everyone thinks with a fixed mindset now and then. Consider the advice Dweck (2015) offers after revisiting her original research:

  > How can we help educators adopt a deeper, true growth mindset, one that will show in their classroom practices? You may be surprised by my answer: Let's legitimize the fixed mindset. Let's acknowledge that (1) we're all a mixture of fixed and growth mindsets, (2) we will probably always be, and (3) if we want to move closer to a growth mindset in our thoughts and practices, we need to stay in touch with our fixed-mindset thoughts and deeds.

Praise

Praise is a bit tricky; it can have counterintuitive outcomes depending on what type you use. It can take one or two forms, *process* praise or *person* praise (Haimovitz & Dweck, 2017). Kyla Haimovitz and Carol S. Dweck (2017) tested these types of praise. *Person* praise focuses on an accomplishment: "Nice, you did really well. You got eight of ten on the rubric. That's a tough score to beat." This type of praise *seems* to build a student's sense of competence, but it can lead to task avoidance because it centers on the outcome. Students might view that as tied to their intelligence.

The proper kudos is *process* praise. It is slightly different from person praise and more effectively builds growth mindsets. This type can lead a student to believe that the *process* is how you can improve. When you convey it, you communicate that hard work, not an innate ability, is what produced the result. Using process praise in the classroom is correlated to higher levels of learning (Haimovitz & Dweck, 2017).

There's a caveat to process praise. You have to *connect the work a student did to a learning outcome*, no matter how small: "Nice! You must have really worked hard on that paper. You got seven of ten on the rubric." Praising hard work alone debilitates struggling students because it communicates that they didn't actually make growth with all of their efforts (Haimovitz & Dweck, 2017). If a teacher praises effort alone, the connection between work and intelligence growth will be broken and the teacher could lose that struggling student. See table 2.1 for examples.

Always connect the effort or strategy to an outcome (Haimovitz & Dweck, 2017).

TABLE 2.1: Person Versus Process Praise

Person Praise	Process Praise
"I thought your drawing was better today." (Outcome)	"I saw you putting in a lot of time working on the creature's eyes. Your final product shows improvement." (Effort and outcome)
"You did much better on this test. You scored 90 percent." (Outcome)	"I saw how much more attention you paid and the effort you made in class. Your score went up to a 90 percent." (Effort and outcome)
"I like how hard you're working." (Effort)	"I like how you spent time reviewing the lab experiment, and I see how the job you're doing reflects growth." (Effort and outcome)

*Visit **go.SolutionTree.com/instruction** for a free reproducible version of this table.*

Communication With Parents

Parents are powerful allies when developing a growth mindset in students. Unfortunately, many times they can unintentionally lead their children in the opposite direction. Parents who focus on grades more than learning push a fixed mindset; although, research has some very good news about a teacher's ability to help parents build growth mindsets in their students (Moorman & Pomerantz, 2010, as cited in Haimovitz & Dweck, 2017). How we frame complex learning tasks in our classrooms impacts parents greatly. When we send letters or emails to parents that say a challenging task is about developing a skill and not measuring a fixed ability, parents demonstrate less focus on outcomes, less controlling behavior, and more positive influence on their children (Moorman & Pomerantz, 2010, as cited in Haimovitz & Dweck, 2017).

I saw this a lot as a football coach. Parents were very vocal during (and after) games. I recognized two distinct kinds of parents and guardians. One kind made their children hate football, and the other fostered a love for the game. For the first group, they viewed their children's abilities through how well they performed on a single snap or down. If a child dropped the football or missed a tackle, the parent reacted with disgust. The other group viewed every snap and down as a positive step toward learning more about the game. Even when things did not go their team's way, they stayed positive. It was clear they did not view the play, game, or even the season as the reason for playing. Learning lessons like teamwork, goal setting, and facing challenge was their goal for their children. Their children grew to love the game, and the other children burned out.

Communicate with parents about how to develop their children's growth mindsets. Share the information from table 2.1 (page 33) on how to praise a student. Consider sending communications to parents that give them alternatives to the questions they might typically ask. Table 2.2 has examples of the kinds of alternatives you can share.

TABLE 2.2: Fixed Mindset Versus Growth Mindset Conversations for Parents

Fixed Mindset	Growth Mindset
"How did you do on the test?"	"Did you do your best on the test?"
"You have to do better next time."	"What do you think you can do to learn more for the next test?"
"Did you finish your homework?"	"What did you learn from your homework?"

| "I'm glad that project is finally done!" | "You put in the work on that assessment. All the growing you did will pay off!" |
| "You need to bring your grades up." | "Do your grades reflect how much you're learning?" |

*Visit **go.SolutionTree.com/instruction** for a free reproducible version of this table.*

Schools use many different parent communication systems, including those that send a short text message to parents. Each week, or after a test or project, consider sending a growth-minded question to parents and guardians that they can then ask their children.

The Power of *Yet*

Yet is a very powerful little word for all of us. Its simplicity is matched by its deep meaning. I suggest all teachers put up huge posters on the walls of their classrooms that say only one thing: *YET*. Say it often in your class. Model it and live it in your own life!

To understand the importance of *yet*, consider how it changes the following sentences.

- "I can't understand fractions (yet)."
- "I haven't finished my project (yet)."
- "I can't read well (yet)."

Communicate the power of *yet* in your classroom with a simple exercise. Ask students to explain their thinking, even when they are wrong. Students don't see errors as necessary to the learning process (Fisher et al., 2016), but working with them to explain their thinking even when it contains errors is a powerful reflection activity that helps students develop growth mindsets. Do not let wrong answers hold a stigma in your class; find them intriguing. That openness communicates the importance of open-ended, growth-oriented thinking and confirms to students that you are invested in them reaching their goals. It shows that you believe in their *yet*.

Formative Assessment Strategies

Some formative assessment strategies, especially those that do not allow students to opt out of giving information, are helpful for your least engaged students (McNeece, 2019). These strategies get students to think on their feet, evaluating their own competence—sometimes moment to moment.

Formative assessment isn't a new concept in education. Educators have written entire books about how and when to use formative assessment. With that said, I share the following strategies because everyone can benefit from reminders. I see formative assessment occurring in many classes, but despite it being widely accepted as best practice, it isn't an educational norm in every classroom. This section has some of my favorite strategies. Pick two or three that you aren't already using and practice them for a week.

Feedback

What makes feedback effective? Education expert Grant Wiggins (2012) says feedback is best when it includes the following seven characteristics.

1. **Goal-referenced:** It should refer to what students are working toward achieving: a skill or an understanding, for example.

2. **Tangible and transparent:** The student should know what taking that feedback into account in future work will result in.

3. **Actionable:** It should tell students how to get where they're going. It isn't simply an observation. When you're done giving a bit of feedback to a student, he or she knows what to do next.

4. **User-friendly:** Students need to be able to understand the feedback before they can reflect and act on it.

5. **Timely:** The more recent the event on which they're getting feedback, the more effective the feedback is. Sometimes it's tough to return feedback quickly when the student's work is substantial, but providing verbal feedback throughout that work (see the *ongoing* characteristic) will help.

6. **Ongoing:** Effective feedback is ongoing throughout the learning process. The feedback guides students; it doesn't judge their results or efforts, and it doesn't comment on the learning only a single time. Effective teachers build checks for understanding into the routine (Mangiante, 2011).

7. **Consistent:** This means having the same expectations for everyone, so that the actions they're taking are moving everyone toward the same goal. Rubrics come into play here, so feedback and assessment are standardized.

Consider these aspects when providing feedback, too.

- **Delivery method:** You can give feedback in multiple ways. You can tell a student. You can write on a sticky note. Even a thumbs-up is feedback. The key is to figure out which works best for each student.

- **Focus:** Focus on the positive. Giving negative feedback does not produce positive results. You can point out an issue to correct, but it always needs to be framed as a quick step to get back on target (the outcome). In attempting to build competence, share with students when you see them succeeding. As mentioned, make sure it is process praise (page 33).

- **Description:** Students do not want their work or efforts judged. Be descriptive, avoiding vague "good job!" and "this needs work" statements, and always point out a positive along with whatever you have identified that needs to change. Feedback should be process-based, not personal, to reinforce certain specific academic-boosting behaviors (Orkin et al., 2018). An improvement strategy in the offered feedback is crucial.

- **Connection:** When students can connect prior knowledge and prior effective learning strategies when they're exploring new concepts or problems, it builds competence. Point that out when you see it. When students develop mental systems that first tap into their current understandings and previous experience, and then identify their own most effective ways to begin learning new concepts the next time, they are building competence.

- **Who and when:** You can give feedback to a student, group, or the entire classroom. Understand that one student's misconception might also be held by others, so when you encounter a feedback experience that was helpful for that student, consider delivering the message to the entire class. You can give feedback when you're walking around the room, speaking to a group, or during a one-to-one meeting, also. Feedback comes from both sides, so accept feedback from students.

Teachers cannot give meaningful feedback without knowing where their students are and where they need to go. Knowing your students—you can see where related-ness comes into play—helps you see their current skills. Teachers must consider the knowledge and understanding the student brings to the situation (Ng et al., 2018).

It is also important to mention that the forthcoming Cooperative Learning for Competence section (pages 45–49) has many formative assessment strategies. While classmates are talking to one another is a great time to listen and give feedback and, when you model it, students will give the same kind of feedback themselves.

Increasing feedback in the classroom can happen tomorrow. Doing so will help develop your students' sense of competence.

Consensograms

Consensograms come in many forms. Sometimes they are posters or electronic projections. They are usually some type of large graphic organizer that all students have to come and put their opinions, thought, or answer on to. Sometimes these are yes or no charts with stickers, and other times they are elaborate pictures at the front of the room that students put sticky notes on to communicate what they know, think, or feel about something. Consensograms make students get out of their seats to share some aspect of their understanding and make the thinking in the room visual.

Next time you are teaching a new topic, consider having one up so students can see it as they come in. The consensogram can be a simple one-to-ten scale, with one being low and ten being high. Give the students sticky notes on which they write their names and then place under the number they think correlates with their knowledge on the new topic. After everyone has placed the sticky notes, you can ask students who have previous knowledge to share what they know. Students can move their sticky note after each day. They will see their competence grow!

Four Corners

Students vote with their feet during this strategy. By labeling the four corners of your classroom 1, 2, 3, and 4, you turn your room into a visual scale for your students. They can stand up and move around to show how well they think they understand a topic. Or, they can answer multiple-choice questions this way: "Think about which answer, one through four, is correct. Then move to that corner and tell someone there *why* you think that is the correct answer." Teachers can also create a scale. For example, a high school biology teacher may ask, "How comfortable are you dissecting the fetal pig?" and an elementary teacher may ask, "Did you agree with the character choices? Four means you totally agree, three means you kind of agree, two means you disagree a little bit, and one means you totally disagree. When you get there, tell the other people in that corner why you chose that level." Consider having each student discuss their perceptions while in their groups. You can move through groups to listen and give feedback.

Hand Signals

Hand signals including thumbs-up or -down and fist to five (DuFour et al., 2016) instantly help you take the temperature of a class's learning. For thumbs-up or -down, just ask students if they understand a concept. Scan the room to see who has it, who hasn't gotten it yet, and who needs to indicate one way or another. Fist to five is a variation with answers based on a scale. A fist is the lowest level of understanding; all five fingers up indicates complete understanding. When you use hand signals for formative assessment, you can make your way to the people or groups that need feedback to stay on target. This strategy helps students not feel lost; it lets you provide additional support, which can maintain their feeling of competence.

You can ask them the same question at the beginning and end of class. As a teacher, I used fist to five many ways, but the most helpful was checking with students working in groups to see how much longer they thought they needed to finish a task. The visual told me how many more minutes they needed, but it also helped me see which groups got it and which needed more support from me.

Exit Tickets

If you want to leave the class, you have to turn in a ticket on your way out the door! This common strategy asks students to reflect on the day's lesson and provide a response to some kind of prompt. Something like two stars and a wish encourages metacognition—students write two things they learned that day and one thing they want to learn in the future. When this is the classroom norm, students begin to expect to answer those questions as the class proceeds and apply their thinking in the moment to this expectation. It also allows them to see how they grew during class, making it clear that their effort increased their knowledge. Not only does this grow their feelings of competence, but it also allows you to target supports.

On their way out of class, you can even use process praise based on what students wrote: "Your effort today really led to this breakthrough!"

Props

Props create a change of pace in class. Consider having a bell like those found at a front desk of a hotel that, when pivotal learning happens, a student rings the bell. When he was teaching high school English, now-administrator Parker Salowich II moved the bell into different places around the room during a lesson to keep everyone on their toes and started the bell with a different student each day (P. Salowich, personal communication, August 20, 2019). The real assessment isn't about a student ringing the bell at a specific time, but about acknowledging an important point, like a character's experience that prompted growth, was made. If they missed it, you can give immediate feedback.

Similar to the consensogram, you can tape three small pieces of stock paper—one red, one yellow, and one green—to the front of each student's desk, and clip a clothespin onto the red paper. Allow students to move their clothespins from red to yellow to green as they gain understanding. (This works with red, yellow, and green plastic cups, too. Students put the cup that corresponds with their understanding level on top of the stack.) This encourages metacognition, where students are checking in with themselves and assessing their own understanding, which helps to increase competence (Desautel, 2009). You can occasionally start asking, "What color paper do you think you're on right now?" and move about the room and give feedback to those in need. When students know there is support from the teacher and classmates, it encourages competence and classroom engagement (McNeece, 2019).

For a fun and interesting variation, this formative assessment strategy also allows you to find partners for a collaboration between students. If you cannot give feedback in the time allocated, allow students with greens to find and help students with the yellows and reds.

These strategy variations work in all classes in all grades. It may be true that sometimes older students may be reluctant to expose their need for help, but this is why it is critical to develop and use the strategies. For middle and high school, consider having everyone start on red and move up from there, so no one feels like they are calling attention to themselves. If a student is consistently selecting or staying on red, consider prepping or frontloading him or her at lunch or after school, so when the class meets next, he or she can show competence.

Draw It

Drawing is not just for art class anymore. This approach, by Terry Heick (2017), has students tapping into the right sides of their brains. After talking about a complex part of a lesson, stop and ask students to draw, in ninety seconds, a picture of what you are talking about. You can scan for comprehension as you walk around the room or have students hold up their pictures, then give feedback as needed. The teacher can provide instant feedback to those who need it or reteach if students missed something in the lesson. Students love the change of pace, and this works whether you are talking about ionic bonds in high school chemistry or making friends in kindergarten.

Technology Tools

You can find free formative assessment tools online for all grade levels. Kahoot! (www.kahoot.com), Quizlet (www.quizlet.com), and Quizlet Live (www.quizlet.live)

let students use smartphones or tablets to answer questions, either in groups or individually. Though they get feedback on their answers, these tools only offer feedback on whether a response is correct or incorrect, and what the correct answer is.

Plickers (www.plickers.com) does nearly the same thing, but only the teacher needs a device; the students make decisions using preprinted *plickers*. Students hold up their plickers, and the teacher scans with a phone camera for an instant formative assessment that can be projected in front of the class. This only reveals whether a student has selected the correct answer, but you can use it as a voting system where students share their perceptions. Consider using this tool like you would the red, yellow, and green papers or cups. Students just hold up their plicker, and the data come to the front board in a way that allows them more anonymity. Plickers may be a better option for elementary students or in classrooms where some students simply don't have phones.

Ability Trees and Story Maps

Have you played a video game lately? Have your students? Let me tell you that ability trees are common in video games. They are a progression of small increments that players can see. Based on what they see, students can decide on specific paths to level up (show their experience) in the video game. It helps them to create both short-term and long-term goals for their experience. It helps them prioritize their current activity in the game, too. For example, when my son plays the game *Spider-Man*, he gets to decide what powers and skills that he will have—a special web to shoot or a dive to make from the top of a building. He can't choose all possible skills at once, so he has to plan ahead and level up to get what he wants.

Video game designers have done this for years because it is effective and enjoyable. We can do the same thing in our classrooms. What skills do students need in order to master the learning? Do those skills or understandings have different levels? Consider the ability tree for diagramming a sentence (figure 2.1, page 42), the ability tree for learning basic equations in algebra (figure 2.2, page 42), and the ability tree for hand-building ceramics in fine arts (figure 2.3, page 43).

In the ability tree, students can see the overall goal while they follow a step-by-step progression, like a concept or curriculum map or skills flowcharts. Everything is in small chunks to avoid intimidating learners. Developing these chunks for class can also bring a special clarity to your thinking about content delivery, as a form of backward design (Wiggins & McTighe, 2005). As you develop your unit skill trees, consider building multiple paths. This gives a sense of autonomy (chapter 3, page 55), but it also allows students to return to the learning, which helps them go deeper and connect with the curriculum (chapter 5, page 107). A skill tree helps the teacher point out to a student his or her success along the way.

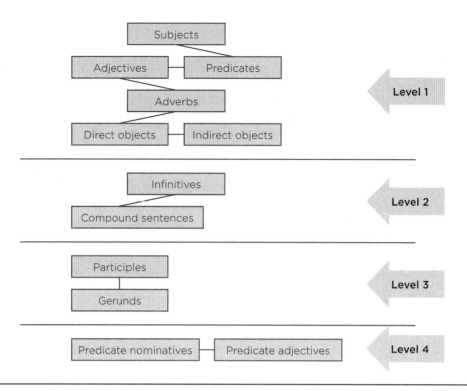

FIGURE 2.1: Ability tree for learning to diagram sentences.

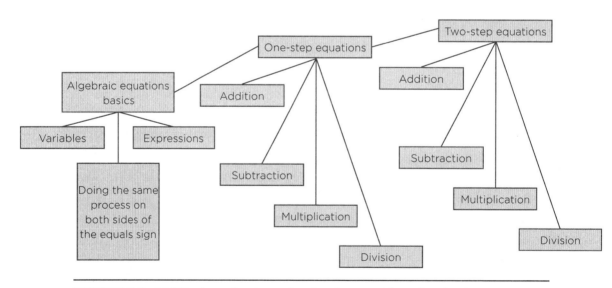

FIGURE 2.2: Ability tree for learning basic equations in algebra.

This approach works because classrooms designed for incremental success help build a sense of competence. Some basic and surface-level learning can engage the students who have a failure-avoidance mindset. These easy steps, or surface-level learning, can help students build confidence (Fisher et al., 2016).

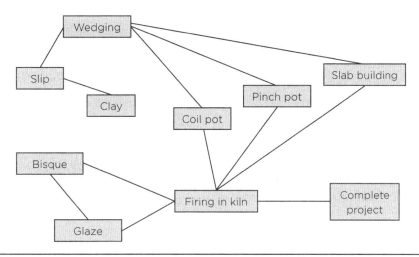

FIGURE 2.3: Ability tree for learning the basics of ceramics.

Because academic self-concept and skill development are reciprocal (Green et al., 2006), as students experience incremental successes, they develop positive academic self-concepts. These positive academic self-concepts are connected not only with that particular skill, but with your class. Be careful though—classrooms that stay with low-level learning tasks debilitate students, but low-level learning is a good place to start for some students (Fisher & Frey, 2015). Disengaged students need highly engaging, small tasks to build them up as we move them toward stronger engagement (McNeece, 2019).

Display ability trees in the classroom so students have visual cues of their growth throughout the year, even after completing a unit. The tree acts as both an artifact of their success and a trigger for memory of that skill. When students can see the learning, it helps them reflect on their learning, allows them to step up to challenges, and helps them cope with setbacks (Orkin et al., 2018).

An ability tree allows for variation that shows student learning maps with the learning target, vocabulary, three key learning blocks, and the lesson's essential questions (Thompson & Thompson, 2009). When one of my teachers had to go home for an emergency, I acted as the substitute in one of the social studies fifth-grade classrooms. The teacher regularly used a student learning map. I was giving the students the assessment and in class after class, the students came in and confidently sat down with the test. I saw many looking over at the student learning map. Their eyes would scan and find what they were looking for. There were no answers on the map, but it triggered their memories. The visual maps scaffolded students who needed the extra support.

Story maps are another variation (Bigelman & Peterson, 2016), and they work in any class from kindergarten to advanced placement literature. Figure 2.4 is an example of the latter, with a story map based on *A Midsummer Night's Dream* (Shakespeare, 1600/1997).

You can build them ahead of time or develop them as students read an assigned book. If you build the story map as you go, it helps maintain the feelings of competence in students who may have missed the reading. Those students can still participate in the discussion and know the main plot developments. If you plot the entire story from the beginning, it helps to assist in overall comprehension of the book,

Hermia, Demetrius, Lysander, and Helena all travel to the woods. Lysander and Demetrius want to fight. After all kinds of drama, Puck, yeah that dude again, finds them and really plays a joke, making both of the guys fall in love with Helena and not Hermia, whom they were originally fighting over . . . total soap opera!

The Mechanicals go to practice in the woods, only to have Puck, that twisted sprite, turn their lead actor, Nick Bottom, into a donkey-headed monster and scare everyone away.

Egeus, one of the king's friends and Hermia's dad, tells his daughter (in front of the king) whom to marry—Demetrius—or she'll have to become a nun. She loves a dude named Lysander and her friend, Helena, loves Demetrius. Hermia and Lysander plot to marry in private. Helena decides to blow that plan up by telling Demetrius, to gain his affection.

Puck gets the special love juice but is quickly distracted by the strange groups of humans he finds in the woods. He proceeds to mess with everyone in some seriously twisted ways!

Duke of Athens Theseus and Hippolyta argue about their forced wedding. Hippolyta's people were conquered by Theseus, and now she has to marry him? Not surprisingly, she's only lukewarm to the idea.

We meet Puck (a naughty fairy), Oberon (king of the fairies), and Titania (queen of the fairies). Oberon and Titania are doing some serious arguing about a boy they both want as part of their crew. Titania leaves, and Oberon and Puck make some seriously wrong plans to play a trick on Titania—some really messed-up stuff.

The Mechanicals, a bunch of hard-working dudes, introduce their play *The Most Lamentable Comedy and Most Cruel Death of Pyramus and Thisbe*. These guys obviously know how to party and entertain the king with their ironic play (#sarcasm)!

Source: Adapted from Shakespeare, 1600/1997.

FIGURE 2.4: *A Midsummer Night's Dream* story map.

Source: © 2019 by M. McNeece. Used with permission.

FIGURE 2.5: *Twilight* **story map.**

like pictures do in a children's book. Figure 2.5 is an example of a story map with pictures, though this is a middle school example based on the book *Twilight* (Meyer, 2005). Seeing the entire book also helps a student deconstruct specific plot events and understand their connections to the entire storyline.

Demystifying what students are going to learn with ability trees allows them to feel competent because they can see the path forward. The layout helps students develop a *learning focus*, where they understand that solving problems and developing new skills are the purpose (Martin, 2003).

Cooperative Learning for Competence

Engagement can be sparked through complex interactions and exchanges between students during their learning (Ng et al., 2018). Cooperative learning is a multidimensional instructional process that supports students, while helping them build positive relationships with the class and the teacher. Cooperative learning is such an important part of building relatedness that I discuss more strategies in detail in chapter 3 (page 55).

The most important reason to use cooperative learning is to benefit a sense of competence. Cooperative learning is when students do the work of learning collaboratively. The use of cooperative strategies during the instruction acts as a safety net for students who don't have high levels of competence and who struggle (Fisher et al., 2011; McNeece, 2019). All students, those who are fully, a little, or disengaged, value social interaction with their peers (O'Toole & Due, 2015). This may feel counterintuitive, but in my classroom experience, students learn as much from one another and from their own processing as they do from direct instruction or minilessons. Making sure that at least a quarter of your classroom experience is cooperative learning will gives students time to *process* the critical ideas and understand before they are expected to fully understand it (Fisher & Frey, 2008). They have to have time to play around with the concepts before they have to transfer the skills or knowledge.

Using cooperative strategies also helps beat gaps (Mangiante, 2011; Muhammad & Hollie, 2012). Research shows that schoolwide interventions focusing on cooperative learning in every classroom have a gap-closing impact on reading and mathematics scores on local and state assessments (Fisher et al., 2011). The following cooperative learning strategies focus on helping students build a sense of competence, but please note that cooperative learning can take many forms, including sustained group work in class. Each of the following strategies can be done in a short amount of time.

Team-Pair-Solo

Follow these six steps for Team-Pair-Solo.

1. Number students into groups of five or six and let them get up and move into their groups.

2. Provide a question or prompt based on current content: an equation to solve or a connection between world events, for example. It can be something the group has to write, say, or do.

3. Let students work with their groups for between five and ten minutes. They should provide evidence that supports their answers. They may even work out an equation on a poster board and, when they find a process that works, leave that artifact up for additional support.

4. When time is up, break students into pairs with people from different groups.

5. Give the partners another five or ten minutes to explain to each other how they solved the problem.

6. Have students return to their seats and individually complete the problem after receiving the support from a team and a partner.

Students who can't complete the work alone will have the support structure to help them provide a correct answer and grow their feelings of competence. Students who understand can help one another. Both of those situations help to build a classroom culture of competence.

Inner Circle and Outer Circle

Inner Circle and Outer Circle activates prior knowledge, boosting a sense of competence as students prepare for an assessment. Follow these four steps.

1. Split your class in half; if you have an odd number, have the larger group form a circle by standing shoulder to shoulder, facing outward.

2. Have the other half of the class form the outer circle, about a foot or two away and facing inwards to a correlating inner circle student.

3. Pose a question—maybe one they will see on the assessment.

4. Give everyone a chance to talk about the answer and rotate the outer circle after two or three minutes, so everyone has a different partner.

   Allow between two and four rotations for every question. That lets students hear and give input to multiple classmates.

Students who do not have a good grasp of the information hear different perspectives from classmates. Plus, after the first rotation, the students who struggle have valuable information to share, a chance to share what they now know, and by doing so, grow a sense of competence.

Give One and Get One

Try these three steps for this activity when you want to get student voices out into the room. This works with all grade levels.

1. The day after you've assigned out-of-class practice, have everyone get out their work when they arrive to class.

2. Instruct each student to take his or her assignment to another student and give that student one problem or question he or she had to work on. Then he or she gets one problem or question from that student in return. They check each other's answers.

3. Have students bounce around to different partners, giving one answer to that partner and asking for one they struggled with. Students can ask others questions like "I couldn't get problem number three, could you?" or "I know how to do problem number seven. Do you need help with that one?"

Students can use this to check their own understanding. Give the students a short amount of time with each rotation, and give them time to process once they get back to their seats. You can use this strategy to provide background on new topics. For example, if your elementary science class is doing a lesson on biology, have the students give one and get one around the room for animals they have at home. You can adapt this strategy many ways.

Numbered Heads Together

Students who lack competence may be reluctant to speak up in class. When you're asking questions and dialoguing with the whole class, consider using this strategy to make sure your struggling learners have support. If your classroom is set up at tables or in rows, you are ready to do this right now. Use the following three steps.

1. Have students number off at the individual tables or desk rows. Each student has a number, and there is a number one at each table.

2. Ask a question and give students several minutes to confer with each other about what they feel is the correct answer. The teacher might ask students to factor a quadratic equation, describe everything they know about magnets, or to name businesses in the community and say what they sell.

3. Call a single number from each table so the student with the corresponding number answers the question aloud.

You can move about the room and make sure students are on target, giving feedback as necessary. When you know a group has nailed the answer, consider calling the struggling student's number and allowing that person to communicate the group's perception and receive the positive feedback for being correct. You can roll a six-sided die to randomize whom you call on, also.

Classroom Interview

Your class is learning some complex things! If students need a quick break, think of using this approach no matter what grade you teach. Ask them to be news reporters by employing the following four steps.

1. Have everyone stand up and walk to a different part of the room to find a partner.

2. Share a variable to differentiate who will be the reporter and who will be the interviewee. You could say the reporter will be the person whose name has the most letters in it, for instance.

3. The reporter asks the interviewee one question: "What could you tell a classmate so she can learn about [*topic the class is working with*]?" This requires student metacognition to identify what challenges them and the best way to figure out how to convey that.

4. After they give their tips, have the pairs reverse roles and pose different questions.

No student can opt out of the learning because everyone is paired, so now everyone has a tip to use when working through the complex task. Go around the room and ask pairs what they came up with, comment on their work and positive thinking, or prompt when something has gone wrong.

Think-Pair-Share

Try the following four-step process.

1. Ask a question or assign a task. Some examples follow. *What is your opinion of the character's actions? What do you think will happen next? Find the triangle's area.*

2. Give students a chance to think independently. How much time you allow depends on the complexity of the question. They can be right-or-wrong questions (to check for understanding), or they can be open ended (for the opportunity to explore feelings about a story or build collective background knowledge). I have seen students write a quick note or solve an equation, and other times I've seen teachers use this just to get students talking.

3. Have students find partners and exchange information. Through this, struggling students who may have the wrong answer are given a chance to check and even change their thinking.

4. Have the groups share their answers or conversation topics.

See-Think-Wonder

See-Think-Wonder is highly effective for developing literacy, especially when students share about a book (Bigelman & Peterson, 2016). The following five steps help build classroom feelings of competence because there are no wrong answers.

1. Ask students a question about a section of a reading, a character, or an event in a story.

2. Have students pair off and report to each other something they notice in the text related to that question.

3. Students answer each other: What do I think about that?

4. Both students answer the final question, "What does it make us wonder?"

5. Ask students to share their ideas with each other and the class. This allows students to think through their own ideas and hear their classmates' thinking.

Reflection Strategies

Collective classroom reflection conversations are very helpful for students who are growing their sense of competence. Those students need an important ingredient they often lack, the vocabulary to discuss their reflections—the *mentalistic vocabulary* (Desautel, 2009). It's helpful to have a classroom discussion where you guide students through think-alouds using mentalistic vocabulary.

Questions and personal journals are ways you can use reflection to build a sense of competence in students.

Questions

Students are always thinking, so helping them focus that thinking with the right questions is helpful. What are the right questions? University of Michigan professor Elizabeth A. Davis (2003) studies middle school students and their science learning. She finds more restrictive questions—but those targeted to spur thinking about specific strategies—actually *inhibit* student reflection. Students who were asked to consider more open-ended questions experienced greater learning.

Davis's (2003) study suggests that generic prompts were more effective than directed prompts, and that the phrase *right now* helps bring students to the moment. Table 2.3 (page 51) compares the directed and general prompts a teacher may have students use in different parts of a lesson.

This is a reminder that overdirecting a student's thinking is not an effective strategy. Every student has a different process, and trying to direct students to think a specific way is not as helpful as just getting them to ask the right questions. How can you ensure in-depth reflection in the classroom? Beyond making sure conversations are happening with the whole class, a great way to implement reflection in your classrooms is with personal journals.

Personal Journals

Journaling for reflection can have multiple uses and serve multiple purposes when it's a reflection tool. You can bring reflection into journaling by having students write about three things: (1) how the content they're exploring connects to their lives (which also boosts relevance, another important aspect of academic self-concept), (2) how the daily activity relates to the unit's bigger picture, and (3) a step-by-step process description of a class activity (Young, 2018). Because journals are artifacts of learning, they help students see how competent they are because of their growth. Refer back to your classroom reflection journals often. Make it a classroom norm;

TABLE 2.3: Directed Prompts Versus General Prompts for Reflection

Part of a Lesson	Directed Prompts for Reflection: Less Effective	General Prompts for Reflection: More Effective
Getting started	"To do a good job on this project I need to . . ."	"What I am thinking about now . . ."
Checking for understanding after reading	"Claims in the article that I did not understand were . . ."	"My thinking right now is . . ."
Checking for understanding after reading	"The evidence I did not understand was . . ."	"What I'm unsure about right now is . . ."
Beginning to write	"To do a good job, I need to . . ."	"Right now, I'm thinking . . ."
During writing	"When I think about how these ideas fit together, I'm confused by . . ."	"What I'm wondering right now is . . ."
After writing	"As I worked through this project, I wish I'd spent more time on . . ."	"My idea right now about my project is . . ."

Source: Adapted from Davis, 2003.

like on the last day of the week, spend time both looking back at the journal and reflecting about the current week's learning.

Terry Heick (2018) provides the following eight prompts that can help students who are in just about any grade connect content to their lives.

1. What surprised you today, and why?
2. What's the most important thing you learned today? Why do you think so?
3. What do you want to learn more about, and why?
4. When were you the most creative, and why do you think that is?
5. What made you curious today? How does learning feel different when you're curious?
6. When were you at your best today, and why?
7. Assuming we were studying the same thing and you could decide and have access to anything, where would you start tomorrow? Why?
8. What can/should you do with what you know?

One of my powerful teaching experiences came from the reflection students did as part of preparing material for a student-led conference. Students in any grade can lead a conference where the student reflects on his or her learning, and, during a conference or celebration, the teacher and parent join the student as he or she talks about it.

Summary

The strategies in this chapter will help develop a sense of competence in students. When that feeling grows, students demonstrate more persistence during challenging tasks. Rachel from the story in the beginning of the chapter demonstrated that persistence. Competence drives persistence in all subject areas because competence develops a student's whole positive academic self-concept. In the beginning of the chapter, you see Rachel's teacher communicate his belief in her abilities. Reflect on your own feelings about your students' competence. A teacher's perception of a student's competence impacts that student (Haimovitz & Dweck, 2017). In classroom cultures that support competence, students grow their love of learning. Use the "Teacher Self-Assessment Rubric—Competence" reproducible (pages 53–54) to evaluate your classroom's competence-building culture.

Teacher Self-Assessment Rubric—Competence

Use this rubric to identify the research-based strategies that you implement in your classroom and those that can help you in your classroom tomorrow.

	4—Exemplary	3—Meets Expectations	2—Developing Skills	1—Emerging Understanding
Growth Mindset (pages 30–35)	• I display positive, authentic artifacts related to growth and fixed mindsets. • I consistently use process praise. • My teacher-to-home connection and growth mindset programs are evident.	• I display artifacts that reflect growth and fixed mindsets. • I use process praise. • I intervene to help establish growth mindsets.	• I display artifacts related to growth mindset. • I sometimes use growth-mindset language. • I use praise but don't reference growth.	• I don't promote or discuss growth mindset. • I don't address mindsets. • I use person praise.
Formative Assessment (pages 35–50)	• All seven major elements of best-practice feedback are identifiable when I give feedback. • Feedback positively impacts learning and helps students push through challenges. • I weave multiple types of formative assessment into lessons.	• Feedback is within the just-right level of support. • I use formative assessment daily. • I use various formative assessment activities. • My presence and comments positively impact student learning.	• I use feedback topically and may miss one or more of the best-practice elements. • I cannot give all students feedback or, if I do, it is surface level. • I sometimes use formative assessment, but it is surface level or disconnected from the learning.	• I refrain from positive feedback. • I give formative assessments intermittently, or I do not implement any formative assessment.

page 1 of 2

Ability Trees and Story Maps (pages 41–45)	• Ability trees from present and past learning are displayed in class or the hallway. • Students and I refer to collections of student work. • Students regularly interact with visible learning guides.	• An ability tree or story map is displayed. • Students are clearly connected to or accessing displayed information.	• An ability tree or other student work is displayed, but the artifact is still in development or students don't use it.	• I have not displayed artifacts showing learning growth.
Cooperative Learning (pages 45–49)	• I consistently use cooperative learning twenty-five percent of the time or more. • I use various cooperative activities, and student participation is evident.	• I use cooperative learning almost twenty-five percent of the time. • I use one or two cooperative activities, and students participate.	• I use cooperative learning less than twenty percent of the time. • Students generally comply with cooperative activities but are not enthusiastic or don't understand their purpose.	• I rarely use cooperative learning, or avoid it altogether.
Reflection (pages 50–52)	• In my class, students consistently use self-reflection artifacts. • I intentionally ask proper questions and devote time to student growth.	• I prompt self-reflection during every unit, sometimes as whole-class conversations. • I ask questions to promote deeper thinking.	• I prompt self-reflection topically or occasionally. • I don't intentionally ask proper questioning strategies.	• I do not prompt self-reflection.

CHAPTER 3

AUTONOMY

Mrs. Johnson's eighth-grade mathematics class slope project was due on Friday. Everyone had to create a representation of an equation of a line. Currently, Gerri had two ideas on how to get the slope done—either use glue and popsicle sticks or ask her uncle to cut a piece of wood.

On her way out of class, Gerri unintentionally said out loud, "If I call my uncle, and he doesn't get back to me right away, I might be late with the project."

Mrs. Johnson heard her and said, "Good thinking. I'm sure your uncle is dependable, but is there another way you could get the project completed?" She was asking Gerri to push her own thinking.

"Well, my uncle could cut a piece of wood that I draw the angle on. I just have to make sure he has wood and the time to do that for me. I could also just find three popsicles and use those, but it may be a little harder to create the proper slope that way. I would need a ruler for that. I'm not sure I have one at home."

Mrs. Johnson assured her, "You're on the right path. And making different plans, just in case one doesn't work out, is really good strategizing."

The bell rang, and the students filed out. Gerri wrote popsicle eating as homework in her planner.

While walking to her next class, Gerri saw the sixth graders playing around in the hallway. She shook her head and continued on, thinking about when she was a sixth grader. Her grades had been very different this year. "I didn't do a great job of keeping my planner back then," Gerri thought as she glanced down at the planner she was carrying. She felt in control of what she was going to do to finish the project. "Popsicles it is," she thought!

• • • • • • • • • • • • • • • • • • • ♥ • • • • • • • • • • • • • • • • • • •

How can we put students in command of their learning—give them autonomy—and still retain necessary order? An autonomous student can see where he or she is going, showing higher self-efficacy behaviors (Green et al., 2006; Martin, 2003), such as planning accordingly, tracking progress, and increased curiosity and self-esteem

(Harper, 2007). Being able to plan a long-term project with the tools available to her, and making decisions about how to approach a project left Gerri feeling autonomous.

We can break down the elements of autonomy into autonomy-building strategies that lead you and your students to this kind of engagement.

Elements of Autonomy

Autonomy is about feeling in command of your world and being free to make choices. Child psychologist Jean Piaget was the first to conceptualize a student's need to feel in command of his or her learning through autonomy, and Piaget asserted that a student's ability to self-regulate and be an autonomous learner should be an education goal (as cited in Sheffield, 2017). An update of Hattie's (2012) *Visible Learning* research finds that Piagetian Programs—focusing on developmental thinking and allowing students the independence to develop their own thoughts—are the second most effective instructional strategy for student achievement (Waack, n.d.).

In secondary school, autonomous students stay organized and manage their studying well, including knowing where to study (Martin, 2003). These are the behaviors of a student with a positive academic self-concept, and positive academic self-concept is our goal as we develop cultures that foster autonomy.

The autonomy scale has two ends: (1) command and (2) low control. Students with low control do not have a clear picture of what success looks like or the ability to conceptualize what they can do to succeed. They are stuck, and it's frustrating to have so little control over what, when, where, and how they learn (Rubin, 2012). Have you asked your own child what he or she is going to learn at school in the coming week? He or she probably didn't know because the traditional school structure doesn't show students their learning paths ahead of time. It is as if they are strapped in on a roller coaster with no way to control their futures. We can change this to help students feel in command of their learning, to ensure we hear and act on their choices and feelings, and to provide multiple paths to demonstrate learning (Orkin et al., 2018).

The opportunities for autonomy that a teacher builds into a classroom matter. There's a big space between anarchy and authoritarianism, and where a teacher sits predicts how motivated students are, because students show more motivation in autonomous situations (Harper, 2007). Students must have autonomy to experience the intrinsic motivation to learn (Ryan & Deci, 2000b). It's easy to list behaviors that squash autonomy and use them as a list of *don'ts* (Sheffield, 2017).

- Don't dominate talking time in the classroom. Students, especially students at risk, engage more when teachers talk less.

- Don't decide on learning materials without student input. Let them choose a path to the essential learning with options that connect to their personal interest.

- Don't give answers before giving students a chance to think. They need wait time.

- Don't give directives that offer no context. Instead, offer rationales for why something is happening.

- Don't criticize student-generated questions and ideas (though that doesn't mean avoiding effective feedback about them).

- Don't use praise as a reward or use praise instead of feedback.

How do these behaviors intersect with your experiences as a teacher and as a student? How do we develop classrooms that ignite and support autonomy? At the classroom level, teachers develop autonomy three ways: (1) organizationally, (2) procedurally, and (3) cognitively (Stefanou, Perencevich, DiCintio, & Turner, 2004). The following list offers some options of these three ways.

- Support students choosing how to practice with concepts and allow for multiple paths to demonstrate learning targets (procedural, prompting student choice).

- Use cooperative learning that specifically focuses on building autonomy (cognitive, autonomy to work toward the learning).

- Share decision-making power in the classroom (Orkin et al., 2018; organizational culture building).

- Use and support autonomous language (Adler, Schwartz, Madjar, & Zion, 2018; Reeve & Jang, 2006; procedural, prompting student voice).

- Provide planning and study-management help (Farrington et al., 2012; cognition).

Organizational Autonomy

Organizational support comes from how the classroom functions. Autonomy can be built into a class when a teacher works with students to create the rules, jobs, and the everyday processes that allow a classroom to run as a democratic group. When students contribute this way, it becomes *their* classroom. They have actively created their culture, and that is empowering.

Procedural Autonomy

The second key autonomy support is procedural. This is where students have command over the types of assignments they do and even how they are assessed. A classroom culture should amplify student voices and ensure that students not only get to voice their opinions and ideas, but that the teacher follows up with actions on hearing student opinions and ideas. This is an autonomy-building strategy that engages students (McNeece, 2019), and when students have a classroom where rules, assignments, and grades are student-initiated with shared input from adults, they have the highest level of autonomy and command (Hart, 1992). Such classrooms use student perspectives and frequently promote self-initiation of learning (Sheffield, 2017).

Cognitive Autonomy

Students must have their cognitive autonomy supported. Traditional teaching dictates that there is just one right answer and we need students to get to it so we can move on (Robinson, 2009), but that is not deep learning. The Common Core Mathematical Practices (National Governors Association Center for Best Practices [NGA] & Council of Chief State School Officers [CCSSO], 2010b) and the Next Generation Science Standards (NGSS Lead States, 2013) stress cognitive autonomy and the sociocultural nature of learning that I highlighted in this book (Sheffield, 2017), yet we often take the existence of student freedom of thought for granted instead of making sure it is a reality in our classrooms. Consider how much richer understanding and how much greater its staying power when students use their own thinking to achieve a learning target. Teachers that support student cognitive autonomy allow students to find multiple solutions to problems, be independent problem solvers, and even debate ideas within student-centered discussions (Sheffield, 2017).

Autonomy-Building Strategies

Autonomy-supportive behaviors are what teachers do when they provide choice in the activities of learning, allow for self-directed learning, know the students' opinions of what they want to learn, and make learning relevant while reducing the pressure or demands typically associated with a person in authority (Grolnick, Ryan, & Deci, 1991; Skinner & Belmont, 1993, as cited in Sheffield, 2017).

SCHOOLWIDE AUTONOMY SUPPORT

It is important for school principals to build autonomy for teachers, too. Schools with low teacher autonomy have lower student autonomy (Marshik, Ashton, & Algina, 2017), and autonomy is a factor in relatedness and career satisfaction (Warner-Griffin, Cunningham, & Noel, 2018). Teachers need the opportunity to influence policy development during the school-improvement process, to develop intervention programs to help the students whom they see are falling behind, and to choose their professional development opportunities.

How can a principal provide the autonomy that teachers need while delivering the leadership they deserve? Consider the concept of simultaneously tight (nondiscretionary) and loose (discretionary) leadership, which is a hallmark of a professional learning community (DuFour et al., 2016). As part of core instructional strategies (Tier 1 of response to intervention) to raise engagement, principals should follow these guidelines (DuFour et al., 2016).

- Teachers have the autonomy to decide to be on a school-improvement team and who leads that team. I recommend a staff member or a pair of staff members lead the team. The school-improvement process timelines, need for an agenda (but not what's on it), and open participation (including parents) are nonnegotiable.

- Teachers have the autonomy to take what data say and pair those with a research-based approach. Be tight and follow through to make sure their planned Tier 1 strategy is used with fidelity. The school using data and research as part of the school-improvement process is nonnegotiable.

- Teachers have the autonomy to decide what professional development they need. Assigning intervention resources to their intervention strategies and professional development is nonnegotiable. Connect with central office if you don't get funds to do this. School intervention funds, like Title I (Intervention for Struggling Students), Title 2a (Professional Development), and Title III (Supporting English Language Learners) exist.

Skills Practice, Exhibition, and Assessment Choice

Academic choice is an important piece of building an autonomous classroom. Allowing students choice in how they practice skills and demonstrate knowledge is how we do this (Orkin et al., 2018). One can't build an environment that creates intrinsic motivation if students aren't given opportunities to self-direct. This self-direction is the only way to have students build true independence. Let students decide how to explore, test, and transfer their new learning. This is not a new concept. Some educators refer to this choice as differentiation. The teacher's role in a differentiated classroom is highly focused on developing autonomy for the students (Kanevsky, 2011).

Instead of requiring all students to make a presentation or write an essay, for example, allow students to choose among options such as those that follow.

- Give a demonstration.
- Interview an expert.
- Create a song or movie.
- Conduct a game show.
- Moderate a Socratic session.
- Let students decide on test format.
- Use a manipulative.
- Explain their thinking verbally.
- Draw it out.
- Act it out.

Additionally, students must partner with the teacher for both rubric and assessment creation (Desautel, 2009). Letting go like this in the classroom can feel uncomfortable. We have to trust that students can reach learning targets without controlled guidance from us. Research says it's possible, even if we haven't yet gotten there—when autonomy occurs in exploratory learning situations, students have higher motivation to learn; cognitive outcomes don't suffer (Basten, Meyer-Ahrens, Fries, & Wilde, 2014). Many teachers are afraid that if students are left to their own paths, student achievement could fall short. Luckily, this is not the reality.

How can teachers provide autonomy-supportive situations in their classrooms? How can we help put our students in command of their learning? Consistent with the self-efficacy cycle (figure 1.4, page 22), teachers that create an autonomous culture in the classroom have a positive impact on student engagement and motivation (Barber & Buehl, 2012; Furtak & Kunter, 2012), including with a particular group of African American students whom education has traditionally disenfranchised (Gutman & Sulzby, 2000).

Learning Targets

Learning targets are a little different. These learning targets allow a teacher to clearly communicate, track student progress, and celebrate learning (Marzano, 2007). The targets are the small chunks of learning that students will work toward accomplishing that day. The ability trees are the whole pie; the learning target is a single, manageable slice. Learning targets, standards broken into skills with student-friendly language, are best practice; they close engagement gaps (Mangiante, 2011). Chapter 2 introduces ability trees (pages 41–43). One standard may be broken into several learning targets. Make posting these targets a classroom norm so students are aware of what they're expected to know, understand, and do.

Learning targets can be for one day or a few, depending on the length of the lesson. Learning targets help students see the lesson's end goal. Knowledge of the end is something many of us educators take for granted. Clearly stated and posted learning goals have a major impact on student autonomy, because if students know where they need to finish, it is possible for them to plot a course (Dean et al., 2012). Students cannot be in command otherwise. Effective students monitor their learning so they can adjust to achieve the outcomes they must meet (Green et al., 2006; Martin, 2003). This allows them to develop planning and study-management skills. Students can then actively decide if they need to increase time studying or spend additional time on the *stair-step* skills that make up the whole. Self-motivated planning and monitoring boost academic achievement (Martin, 2003). Using smaller pieces allows students to take control of their education.

I can statements say what students can do when they have learned the material, and they are a useful way to post the clearly stated learning targets. If your learning target is full of educational jargon, it won't reach students. Post learning targets or *I can* statements like those in figure 3.1 so your students can understand where they are going.

Standard	*I Can* Statement
CCSS.MATH.CONTENT.6.EE.A.4 "Identify when two expressions are equivalent (i.e., when the two expressions name the same number regardless of which value is substituted into them). *For example, the expressions* y + y + y *and* 3y *are equivalent because they name the same number regardless of which number* y *stands for."*	I can match two equivalent expressions.
CCSS.ELA-LITERACY.RL.3.2 "Recount stories, including fables, folktales, and myths from diverse cultures; determine the central message, lesson, or moral and explain how it is conveyed through key details in the text."	I can give a story's key details that help classmates understand its main message.

FIGURE 3.1: Breaking standards into *I can* statements.

continued ⇨

CCSS.ELA-LITERACY.L.9–10.2.A "Use a semicolon (and perhaps a conjunctive adverb) to link two or more closely related independent clauses."	I can use a semicolon properly.

Source for standard: National Governors Association Center for Best Practices (NGA) & Council of Chief State School Officers (CCSSO), 2010a, 2010b.

The right column provides students with a much clearer picture of what they will be able to do by the end of class. Posting the column on the left will not be helpful to students. *I cans* are quick to develop if you want to put this on your board at the beginning of the day. It just takes a minute to reflect and develop an *I can*. When teacher teams develop *I cans* together, students get a unified picture. Teacher team–created *I can* statements support the teachers themselves; it helps make sure everyone is on the same page.

To take learning targets a step further, consider Fisher et al. (2016). They state that students should also get the following at the beginning of each lesson as part of learning targets.

- Exemplars (teacher-created or from previous students) of different proficiency levels
- Scaled rubrics when co-created with students (Marzano, 2007; see Student-Developed Rubrics, page 69)
- A concept map, flowchart, or skills web of learning progressions (discussed in chapter 2, page 25)

Learning targets allow students to plan and monitor their learning throughout a day. If students have a clear picture of where a class is going, it helps them avoid inefficiency and even the frustration of trial and error (Sadler, 1989, as cited in Beesley, Clark, Dempsey, & Tweed, 2018). For students that struggle in school, learning targets are a critical support. Learning targets help struggling students who are not in command of their learning; they do not identify learning targets on their own (Black & Wiliam, 1998a, 1998b; James et al., 2006, as cited in Beesley et al., 2018).

If you use learning targets, you help produce academic boosting behaviors that will help develop a student's positive academic self-concept. Anchor charts and Know-Understand-Do (KUD) are also forms of learning targets.

Anchor Charts

Think of anchor charts as an expression of the learning that will anchor the lesson. These are small thinking maps created by the teacher and the students that explain where the lesson is going. They are usually done on large poster paper and are about skills that will be the focus during a lesson. Research finds the use of anchor charts to help increase student achievement in elementary and middle school (Fontanez, 2017).

Anchor charts can offer very specific goals that help students target the learning. When developing anchor charts, consider including the following elements (Brown, 2014).

- Use a title and picture to focus students on the topic.
- Color code to help students see different parts or paths.
- Activate student background knowledge.
- Establish a learning target and essential questions.
- Add key vocabulary.
- Feature examples of goals and examples of things that are not goals.
- Organize to help students follow and locate information; don't make it too busy.

When completed, hang your anchor charts as visuals to help connect the learning to the work. An anchor chart becomes an artifact of effective instruction once the lesson is over. If you ever need visually stunning ideas, visit Pinterest (www.pinterest .com) and search for *anchor chart*.

On a related note, researchers Anna V. Fisher, Karrie E. Godwin, and Howard Seltman (2014) of Carnegie Mellon University find that an overly busy classroom can be distracting for the elementary students. This tells us two very important things.

1. Don't overdo the visual stimulation. How much is too much? Use your students' attention as a guide. In the classroom, we hang anchor charts to help the students reference important information, so we expect students to look at the charts. Consider omitting some anchor charts or decorations if students are not able to get back on track and complete their tasks.

2. Engagement is difficult for students during direct instruction. Keep direct instruction brief, and build in more exploratory learning, like the student-directed discussions mentioned earlier. Ideally, your direct instruction should be 25 percent of the learning (Fisher & Frey, 2008).

Know-Understand-Do

Know-Understand-Do tables are another variation of a learning target. The three-column table explains what students should *know*, *understand*, and *do* as they solve a problem built to help learn the target. See the following.

- The *Know* holds the facts, vocabulary, and other basic information.

- The *Understand* column lists the big ideas. These ideas connect to the real world. For example, if the class is studying the United States Constitution's Fourteenth Amendment, the second column might read, *I understand the Fourteenth Amendment's impact on today's society in the United States.*

- The *Do* column combines the knows and understands. These concrete skills are like the *I cans.*

You can use KUD tables to build students' autonomy at all grades, but in my experience, the increased complexity above an *I can* statement makes them especially suited for secondary classrooms.

Cooperative Learning

As you saw in chapter 2 (page 25), cooperative learning is a classroom strategy that helps students in multiple ways. You learned how it helps students grow competence. It also helps students feel more autonomous. During cooperative learning, the teacher transfers the responsibility to learn from the teacher to the students (Fisher & Frey, 2008). This is very different from the traditional model of classroom instruction where the teacher lectures to the students and, immediately after, students work independently.

During cooperative learning times, yes, sometimes students talk off topic, sometimes they play around, and, yes, sometimes they will disrupt the learning of others. With that said, it is important that they learn *how* to cooperatively learn. They will need to work cooperatively with others for the rest of their lives. What a great time it is now to help them acquire this skill.

How can we help students develop into cooperative learners? Even though the student's responsibility increases during cooperative learning, the teacher is not without a role. When the teacher is free to walk the room, listen, and talk with students, it opens new possibilities, including informal assessment and feedback that would not have been available if the teacher just lectured in the front of the room. What the teacher says to the students during cooperative learning matters.

This section elaborates on what the teacher should say as he or she walks around to each group while the class is involved in a sustained cooperative learning segment. Remember, learning is a sociocultural experience (Vygotsky, 1978), and the more tools we give students to communicate ideas and test the ideas of others, the more effective their learning will be (Gillies & Khan, 2008).

During cooperative learning, a teacher's interaction with students enhances the quality of the thinking and problem solving of the student groups (Gillies & Boyle, 2005). As you move about the room, consider using the statements in table 3.1 to drive the collaboration. These specific communications challenge student thinking and promote meaningful engagement (Gillies & Boyle, 2005).

TABLE 3.1: Scaffolding Phrases to Use During Cooperative Learning

Teacher's Action	Teacher's Statement
Icebreaking	"So, what has the group figured out so far? What are we doing here?"
Reflecting	"It sounds as though you are saying . . . ."
Offering suggestions when off track	"Have you thought about . . . ?"
Refocusing on a source	"Did the information we read [or from the source] say anything about this?"
Reframing statements to consider an alternative perspective and redirect back to page	"What I hear you saying is that the group is stuck, but I also hear you saying that the group may have found the solution. What is the solution?"
Validating and refocusing on key elements to find a solution	"You've worked that part out after a lot of effort. I wonder what you may need to do now if you want to find the solution?"
Prompting cooperation	"Do you all agree on that?"
Pushing thinking for evidence	"What is your rationale for doing that?"
Jumpstarting the analysis	"Can you develop a sentence around that?"
Prompting everyone's voice	"Whose solution is that? What other perspectives are there?'"
Reflecting on group dynamics	"This looks really great. You've nearly finished. What percentage of time was the group on task?"
Encouraging leadership	"Was there a group leader today? What did that person do that made him or her a leader? How did that go?"
Saving groups from failure and reflecting on that experience	"The anxiety you feel right now is not permanent. Let's learn from this. How could this work better in the future?" [After student responds] "OK, let's use one of those now."

Source: Gillies & Boyle, 2005.

While your class has the autonomy to work cooperatively, the time you spend cruising the room is extremely important. What you do when they work is a potential booster to their autonomy. Not each group and student will be able to cooperatively work in the most efficient way, but when you help them do so, they adopt your classroom's autonomous culture.

Fisher and Frey's (2008) *Better Learning Through Structured Teaching: A Framework for the Gradual Release of Responsibility* provides a different and student-autonomy-fostering classroom structure. Different than the traditional model for instruction, the structured teaching model, the gradual release of responsibility, breaks teaching into the following four phases.

1. **Direct instruction:** This phase is also known as *I do*. This is where the teacher has all the responsibility, and students have very little autonomy (though a conversational approach to class reduces teacher talk; Fisher et al., 2011). During this time, a teacher may be solving a problem in front of the class, using student input, and explaining the thinking that goes into solving the problem.

2. **Guided instruction during a lesson:** The autonomy has shifted from the beginning of the lesson, when the teacher was in control. This phase, also known as *we do*, is a more interactive time. Students can work in small groups or as an entire class. The teacher and students collaboratively solve and work toward the learning. The teacher usually is the emcee during this part of the lesson, but the students' input becomes a much larger component. The teacher gives feedback to the class, who can see and hear everyone's thinking. That transparency acts as a support as students move toward larger responsibility in their learning.

3. **Cooperative work during a lesson:** This is the *we do it together* part of a lesson, which happens after the teacher and students have worked together. This gives students the chance to explore the learning with their classmates in a self-directed way. This phase is so important because a teacher-dominated class lacks student conversation, which is an essential component of student learning (Dewey, 1933; Livdahl, 1991; Zwiers, 2014). Students need time to explore ideas and each other's connections to the new learning. This is where the students begin to take control over their learning in the lesson.

4. **Independent work:** The final phase is also known as *you do*. Students now have additional time to work on concepts after getting support

from their peers. This is an important time for personal reflection, too. It should also be said that this is not worksheet time nor is it part of an assessment. Consider using journaling (pages 50–52) during this time, to help make the time as student self-directed as possible.

These phases can come in any order the teacher sees fit for a lesson, but each part is important. Consistently using these four phases of a lesson builds the expectation of student responsibility. In my experience, each day during this approach, they get better at accepting their learning roles and responsibilities. Using structured teaching creates a culture where autonomy is the norm.

Student Talk

Student-directed discussions break the norm of sit-and-get, where teachers lead lectures. When students are active in class, their academic achievement goes up (Freeman et al., 2014). In fact, research shows that "exploration proved to be not only more impressive than direct instruction but also more impressive than a combination of the two—suggesting that direct instruction can be not merely ineffective but positively counterproductive" (Dean & Kuhn, 2007, as cited in Strauss, 2017). Teachers who help students by facilitating these situations make this possible.

A good alternative is student-led discussions. Deep discussions take practice, but autonomy is one of the positive driving forces behind this sit-and-get. Education authors Michael S. Hale and Elizabeth A. City (2006) say implementing the following suggestions sets students (and teachers) up for success.

- Have students face each other; their desks or tables should be in a circle or a U shape.

- After someone has posed an initial question or idea, and everyone has had time to think (and maybe write) about it, do a pair share. This increases relatedness and feels safer to students than whole-group sharing when they're just starting a conversation or are inexperienced discussion leaders.

- Use protocols to help frame the discussions. The National School Reform Faculty's Ping Pong protocol (https://bit.ly/2KeMoAL) and Constructivist Learning Groups protocol (https://bit.ly/2wMD9Pk) can help.

- Base the discussions on texts, which include art, maps, music, essays, political cartoons, mathematics problems, and primary documents. These conceptual representations provide a framework. You don't have to limit your materials to texts.

- Balance your focus on content with a focus on process. Students are taking control of the dialogue and their own learning at the same time, and juggling the content of their learning and its process is no easy task. Strauss (2017) recommends following up discussions by asking "How did we do with safety [taking cognitive risks and being empathic] today? How challenging was the conversation?" Assigning students to observe the class and make notes of specific concepts or skills helps, too. Students can look for evidence and build on ideas.

Autonomy is in students' sight when they lead discussions.

Student-Developed Classroom Constitution

Good classroom management is important, but I would argue that self-directed students come more from what we do to build a community and less from orderly but iron-fisted authority. In the traditional educator mindset, students are there to listen and do. This is not how we build students' autonomy. Instead, let your classroom be a model for democracy. Building a classroom behavior and academic constitution helps students feel in control of their learning (Muhammad & Hollie, 2012; Orkin et al., 2018). Also, Constitution Day is September 17, early in the school year. This is a perfect day for rolling out this classroom document.

Student engagement increases when students participate in developing classroom rules (Harper, 2007). Begin by writing collaboratively (sort of like that preceding the United States' Constitution). This is an example in the form of a preamble (like that preceding the U.S. Constitution) and is something students can work on together to complete (Creative Educator, n.d.). A teacher may have a brief discussion about the preamble and then break the students into cooperative teams to develop their own preamble. Each group can share their thinking. From there, the teacher can build a summary of the class suggestions, and the class can vote on whether to have these be the rules that guide their own behavior.

"We the students of _____ class, in order to form a more perfect union, establish _____, insure _____, provide for _____, promote _____, and secure _____, do ordain and establish this Constitution for our classroom."

The students can also develop a bill of rights. What are the rights of the students and teacher in the classroom? Begin by asking students the following types of questions.

- "What are our goals?"
- "What behaviors do you expect of other people in our classroom and of yourself?

- "How will I support you?"
- "How will you support me?"
- "What will a typical day in class be like?"

These can be the foundations of trust, safety, and the relationships you begin building with students, too. Therefore, this strategy will help relatedness, as explained in chapter 4 (page 79).

These questions and others that come up will provide an excellent way to discuss the expectation in your class. Identify the ideal rights for everyone and even establish what will happen when these rights are violated. This empowering activity is about giving your students command over the classroom.

Student-Developed Rubrics

Students who do not feel in control of their learning have a difficult time understanding what they can do to improve (Martin, 2003). Developing classroom rubrics for grading helps students see what it takes to accomplish the learning. They provide a predetermined, mystery-free measure of success (Kinne, Hasenbank, & Coffey, 2014). Students learn better when given rubrics (Brookhart, 2013), and rubrics are another way to monitor learning, understand mistakes and misconceptions, and offer meaningful corrections (Soiferman, 2015). Rubrics give students the questions they need to ask themselves about their thinking, thereby using metacognition (Bolton, 2006; Jonsson & Svingby, 2007, as cited in Kinne et al., 2014), which is a telltale behavior of a self-efficacious student.

Rubrics also help teachers give more effective feedback (Andrade & Du, 2007; Diab & Balaa, 2011, as cited in Kinne et al., 2014). When students are partners in creating the rubrics, teachers are developing autonomy (Hart, 1992; McNeece, 2019). Students like rubrics too. They reported having a higher quality of work and the ability to more clearly communicate about an assignment when a rubric is available for an assignment (Reynolds-Keefer, 2010, as cited in Kinne et al., 2014). There are factors that allow a student to be in command of their learning.

To begin developing an assignment's rubric, teachers need to do a little prep work prior to involving students. The following four steps provide a helpful beginning to this process.

1. Identify exemplars for what your students' work will be. Have multiple exemplars ready to show students. In English class, these may be papers written by students in previous classes. In art class, this

may be a piece that you are using to help demonstrate a strategy. In mathematics class, this may be a complete performance task where students use all of the different required elements.

2. Identify the criteria that the exemplars display. For example, if students are writing an essay, the use of a thesis statement would probably be an important criterion to add to your rubric.

3. Have a conversation with students in which you break down an assignment's elements or criteria. Explain the key components of what you expect. If a rubric exists, for example, from a science-based response, you would explain scientific phenomena, key vocabulary, and the evidence required for exhibiting proficiency. Keeping that number of criteria to a maximum of five is best; that helps keep students from feeling overwhelmed.

4. After deciding the number of elements or criteria, with students, determine the number of levels in your rubric. Typical rubrics have four proficiency levels: 4—Exemplary, 3—Meets Expectations, 2—Developing Skills, and 1—Emerging Understanding.

Rubrics have the following four basic parts (Yale, n.d.). Figure 3.2 shows these parts.

1. A description of the assignment
2. The criteria that are being evaluated
3. The different proficiency levels
4. A description of those levels

Explain the rubric's format and crowdsource its development in your classroom. The time that it will take to develop the rubric is worth it. Begin with Meets Expectations and work through the descriptions of each level, moving to levels 1, 2, and 4 next (if that's how many levels you and students agree on). Students enjoy stretching their thinking to come up with their spicy-hot goals for the Exemplary level. The students' input is the key. They are creating their own expectations for success while also learning to understand key characteristics to get the grades they want.

Description of the Assignment				
	4—Exemplary	**3—Meets Expectations**	**2—Developing Skills**	**1—Emerging Understanding**
Criterion 1	*(Exemplary description)*	*(Meets Expectations description)*	*(Developing description)*	*(Basic description)*
Criterion 2	*(Exemplary description)*	*(Meets Expectations description)*	*(Developing description)*	*(Basic description)*
Criterion 3	*(Exemplary description)*	*(Meets Expectations description)*	*(Developing description)*	*(Basic description)*
Criterion 4	*(Exemplary description)*	*(Meets Expectations description)*	*(Developing description)*	*(Basic description)*

Source: Adapted from Yale, n.d.

FIGURE 3.2: A basic rubric layout.

Visit **go.SolutionTree.com/instruction** *for a free reproducible version of this figure.*

To do this, in a guided instruction format, use students' ideas during class to create bulleted items for each criterion starting at Meets Expectations. Possibly allow them to label the 4, 3, 2, and 1. If my own children labeled these, level 4 would be *Sick* and level 1 would be *Lame*. Allow students to discuss what exactly constitutes an exemplar and so forth down the scale. This is a perfect opportunity to use the cooperative activities that have students talk out their thinking aloud. Finally, showing them exemplars and asking them to identify and articulate what makes it a specific level can help reinforce the ideas and encourage metacognition as well.

It is realistic to expect a student or two to attempt to stack the deck either for or against the class. Make sure you have thought through what your expectation might be. Be forewarned, though, that your students will probably expand your thinking on what qualifies work as an exemplar. Also remember, no matter how it begins, the final product will provide ownership for the students. Refer to it regularly, especially when you have a student who may have been out sick the day the rubric was generated. The level of control that a collaboratively developed rubric provides students will impact how self-determined they become and how deep they go during their skills practice.

Autonomous Language

What a teacher says in the classroom matters. Our language is a cultural norm, as it both represents and helps create a classroom's culture. We can gauge how empowering a teacher is by knowing the words he or she uses and whether it encourages autonomy. Through modeling and leadership, we construct the norms, artifacts, and language in our classrooms (Adler et al., 2018). Consider how you talk to your students. Do your words create a sense of autonomy for them? If so, wonderful. If not, the good news is that you are in control of that language, and changing how you speak is within your control. Furthermore, the communication norms you model in your class will transfer to your students as they work together.

Student-friendly language is part of the necessary language that allows autonomy, and comprehending learning targets and assessment language is crucial to their work. In the classroom, teachers who foster autonomy communicate in a non-evaluative, flexible, and informational way (Adler et al., 2018; Reeve & Halusic, 2009). Table 3.2 offers eight situations and instructional phrases that teachers can use to build autonomy (Adler et al., 2018; Reeve & Jang, 2006).

TABLE 3.2: Autonomy-Building Phrases for Teachers

Situation	Autonomy-Building Phrase
Acknowledging choice	"What have you decided?" "Whatever you decide, I'm in!"
Asking students to get started on an assignment, focusing on what they want	"Which [*problem type*] do you want to start with?"
Offering hints, expressing that a particular course of action could be helpful	"What if you try holding the puzzle in your hand first? See what you think about it then."
Being responsive to student-generated questions and comments	"That is an interesting observation." "Yes, you have a good point."
Helping a student meet a challenge	"Yes, I know it's a difficult one, but you've got this."
Using optimism to encourage	"There is still thinking to be done here, but I think you are getting close."
Offering feedback while maintaining student command	"I like the first question you wrote, but they are both suitable for the project. Which do you prefer?"
Giving ownership	"Keep thinking about this part of the project, and if your thinking changes, you may want to investigate it."

Source: Adapted from Adler et al., 2018; Reeve & Jang, 2006.

It is also important that teachers consider the autonomy-*destroying* statements we might sometimes use (and acknowledge that we will make mistakes despite our best intentions and efforts). Any phrase that forbids choice, such as those in the following list, is hurtful to a student's feeling of command (Adler et al., 2018; Reeve & Jang, 2006).

- Commands
- *Should* and *ought* statements
- Solutions to problems when students are working through a complex assignment

The comments you make will greatly influence the thinking in your class and are the model for your students' communication with one another. Always speak in a way that builds student autonomy.

Planning and Study-Management Help

When you have succeeded in helping students feel autonomous, how can you empower them with tools to reinforce the behaviors of planning their learning and managing time for studying? When students master these behaviors, they have more positive academic self-concepts, but research does not have many examples of the natural practice that a teacher follows to help students develop strategies for planning and study management (Farrington et al., 2012).

Planning for learning is how students conceptualize how they will work toward success and how they will monitor their progress (Martin, 2003). There are metacognitive strategies that students can create a sort of checklist for. Consider giving a checklist to students at the beginning of a unit and asking them to target these behaviors so they can check off each one. Two checklists follow: one for elementary (figure 3.3) and one for secondary (figure 3.4, page 74).

Am I in Command of My Learning?
❏ I look ahead on the assignment to see what happens at the end.
❏ I make up questions as I read and write them down.
❏ When I don't understand something, I ask the teacher for help.
❏ I write in my planner what I need to do for class.

Source: Adapted from Martin, 2003.

FIGURE 3.3: Elementary learning planning checklist.

*Visit **go.SolutionTree.com/instruction** for a free reproducible version of this figure.*

I'm in Command of My Learning When...
❏ I scan ahead in the book, assignment, syllabus, learning targets, or rubric to see where the teacher is going.
❏ When reading for class, I write down questions to stay focused.
❏ When I don't understand something, I go back and think about it.
❏ I complete my planner each day.
❏ I make tables or lists of what I need to do to learn.
❏ I check back on my planner, book, notes, questions, or lists to make sure I did everything it would take to learn.

Source: Adapted from Martin, 2003.

FIGURE 3.4: Secondary learning planning checklist.

Visit **go.SolutionTree.com/instruction** for a free reproducible version of this figure.

Strong time-management skills require students to use their time at school and away from school effectively (Martin, 2003). This can be difficult for students to manage, but teaching them to consider how things are set up and functioning at home and helping them brainstorm how to be most effective in their studying provide them lots of autonomy when they implement the skills, and the implementation reinforces a positive academic self-concept and the self-efficacy cycle. Finding the proper spot and finding a block of time to work at home are not things that all students, parents, or guardians identify as necessary. Students also need to know that studying outside school can be collaborative. Studying with peers, getting tutoring help, and even going to a library are both fun and productive ways to get in some extra studying.

Give students a chance to think about their own studying and thinking times. I used to create positive routines about where, how, and whom I studied with. Help your students develop their study rituals. In figure 3.5, *work at home* replaces the word *study* to apply to elementary students. For grades 5 and up, which are more likely to have actual homework, consider asking students specifically about studying.

Have students fill out this handout in the beginning of the year and then have them fill it out again later in the year, like at the end of the quarter, to see if they have changed their thinking about studying. Classroom discussions and cooperative learning around the questions in this handout could also be helpful so students can help each other and find possible study partners. Just as we would construct a cooperative learning experience where students can learn content, they can use that time to think about and develop their study rituals.

	Last Year	This Year's Goal	What I'll Do to Meet This Goal
Where do you usually do your work outside of school? (Write all the places you work, and circle the one that you work at the most.)			
How many times do you look at your phone while you're studying?			
Do you listen to music or watch TV while you study?			
Do you make specific goals for studying (either time or topic)?			
For how much time do you usually study after school?			
For how much time do you usually study on the weekend?			
What materials from class do you use when you work at home?			
Outside of school, with whom do you usually do homework?			
What do you do if your given resources don't answer a question or help you study?			

Source: Adapted from Pintrich, Smith, García, & McKeachie, 1991.

FIGURE 3.5: Check students' study management.

*Visit **go.SolutionTree.com/instruction** for a free reproducible version of this figure.*

The purpose is to help students understand how to work on their learning outside of school and figure out how to take command over their learning. Using a chart like this, and spending time working with your students from early grades are very important. Teachers sometimes comment that they do important work with students at school, but that sometimes there is no support at home. The handout addresses that lack of support.

The elementary and secondary learning checklists work (figures 3.3 and 3.4, pages 73 and 74) because they help students build metacognition about their own executive functions. Essentially, they give them data to make decisions about their own autonomy. According to the Harvard Center on the Developing Child (n.d.), executive function has lifelong benefits because it helps us "filter distractions, prioritize tasks, set and achieve goals, and control impulses." These abilities are important to the self-efficacy cycle.

Put your students in command by building their autonomy. *Launching and Consolidating Unstoppable Learning* (McNeece, 2019) has even more strategies, including Socratic seminars, Genius Hour (allowing students to spend devoted time weekly on their own high-interest topics; 20-Time in Education, n.d.), project-based learning, and service-based learning.

Summary

The research suggests the importance of student autonomy, but does the traditional classroom provide actual opportunities for autonomy? Think of the classroom from the Peanuts cartoon where students sit in rows, not moving, listening to a teacher that the audience cannot understand. Think of all of the classroom management classes you had in college. Was the main point about controlling students?

Just like Gerri from the beginning of the chapter, when students have the sense of autonomy developed, it empowers them to develop boosting behaviors like the ability to plan and monitor learning and develop good study management skills. These behaviors reinforce the positive academic self-concepts we are trying to build for all students.

Use the "Teacher Self-Assessment Rubric—Autonomy" reproducible to evaluate your classroom's autonomy-building culture.

Teacher Self-Assessment Rubric—Autonomy

Use this rubric to identify the research-based strategies that you use regularly and effectively and those that can help you in your classroom tomorrow.

	4—Exemplary	3—Meets Expectations	2—Developing Skills	1—Emerging Understanding
Choice Building (pages 59–60)	• I structure daily classroom learning time for exploration. • I consistently support autonomous decisions. • Students take command of their learning and make decisions about their assessments. • I consistently use multiple formats for conveying learning targets.	• Parts of my lessons create an exploratory learning environment. • Standardized assessments exist, but students decide how they are assessed or reassessed. • I post daily learning targets.	• I sometimes let students choose a topic or study method. • All assessments are standardized. • I sometimes post learning targets.	• I don't post learning targets or exploratory artifacts. • All students get the same assignments and assessments.
Cooperative Learning (pages 64–71)	• During cooperative learning, I consistently reflect dedication to connecting with each group. • I consistently use prompts that develop high-quality thinking and problem solving.	• I regularly move around the room and communicate positively with students in a way that adds to learning.	• I use cooperative learning.	• I avoid cooperative learning activities.

page 1 of 2

Student-Developed Constitution and Rubrics (pages 68–71)	• A student constitution and student-developed rubrics from both past and current learning are evident in the classroom. • Students consistently reflect on and consult these tools during class.	• Students have created a constitution and developed rubrics. • Students refer to and use these tools.	• Students created a constitution or developed rubrics with token influence (or I do not use them).	• Students have not developed a constitution or rubrics.
Autonomous Language (pages 72–73)	• I consistently model autonomous communication in a non-evaluative, flexible, and informative way.	• I model autonomous phrases to communicate in a non-evaluative, flexible, and informative way.	• I try to use autonomous comments when it applies to the topic.	• I routinely tell students how to continue working without autonomous language.
Planning and Study Management (pages 73–76)	• My students and intervention systems have planning and study-management checklist artifacts. • Students discuss and refer to the planning and study-management checklists to see how their command of learning has developed over time.	• My students and intervention systems use planning and study-management checklists. • I teach and discuss planning and study management.	• I sometimes use planning or study-management checklists. • I sometimes teach and discuss planning and study management.	• I do not use planning or study-management checklists. • I do not teach or discuss planning or study management.

page 2 of 2

CHAPTER 4

RELATEDNESS

In the hallway outside the classroom, Anthony peeked at his card—the king of diamonds. He could hear the class giggling at another student who had just walked into the room.

Mrs. Hector had dealt three students one card apiece and said to show a corresponding degree of excitement when walking into the classroom. The first student had a three of diamonds and pretended to fall asleep on the teacher's desk. The second student finished his ten of hearts performance with, "Now, let's get learning!"

Mrs. Hector said, "Last but not least, we have Anthony. I wonder how excited he'll be?" Anthony took a deep breath, jumped into the room, and owned the king's role by shouting "OK, it is time to get learning up in here!" He continued, "We are here . . . in the greatest . . . the most amazing . . . class in the schoooooooooool!" Anthony walked back and forth in front of the class. "Can I get a woot woot, y'all?"

There was a brief pause, almost too long, but the class responded with an affirmative "Woot, woot!" They laughed a little, and recognized how out of character Anthony was acting.

"All right teacher, let's get at this," Anthony said and bounded over to his teacher for a fist bump, which Mrs. Hector met. He jumped into his seat and as he landed, Anthony dropped out of character, quietly grabbing his notebook from his book bag.

"That was awesome," Mrs. Hector said. "Class, what card was Anthony?' Hands shot up, and everyone's eyes were on Anthony. He looked around and smiled at the positive attention. Mrs. Hector said, "That was very impressive. You field their guesses and let them know."

Anthony smiled even bigger. Looking back at the class, he thought, "Man, this is fun."

• • • • • • • • • • • • • • • ♥ • • • • • • • • • • • • • • •

We exist in a network, growing from our time spent working with others. I have seen students learn at higher levels when they have solid classroom relationships. I have also seen a lack of connection cause anxiety about school. But relationships are tough. They take work. With that said, situations like the one Mrs. Hector built for her class help students have fun and relate with her, their teacher, and each other. As Vygotsky (1987) says, learning is a social endeavor, so add strategies to your class that initiate and strengthen all of the social relationships.

Humans are predisposed to try to develop meaningful and lasting relationships (Baumeister & Leary, 1995) on a personal and emotional level (Martin & Dowson, 2009). The desire to connect includes the need for positive bonds between teachers and students (Jamison, 2014). Few educators would argue that positive teacher-student relationships are not beneficial to young people's proper growth, achievement, and success at school; the research supports that they are (Martin & Dowson, 2009).

The prevalence of students who have experienced trauma is another factor that impacts relatedness. The educational community is starting to focus on how teachers and administrators can help students who come to school with trauma. *Trauma-informed teaching*, as it is commonly called, is an important strategy for connecting with students who have had traumatic experiences. This practice makes it clear that we have to build relationships with students before they can learn content. Relationship building must be the first priority for these students at risk (McNeece, 2019).

The student in the preceding story, Anthony, has a growing level of relatedness to his teacher and the class because of the relationship Mrs. Hector is building through a very effective strategy. His academic self-concept is shifting through the intense relationship- and trust-building exercise his teacher structured. All students fall somewhere on the relatedness scale on the academic self-concept continuum in figure 1.3 (page 20). Some students are comfortable with relationships, and some are not. Where do your different students fall on the continuum? How do you currently develop a true sense of relatedness in the classroom? What process do you take to help build individual teacher-student relationships? Equally important, how do you monitor your potential bias to make sure all students feel accepted and appreciated, and monitor your own bias so you don't unconsciously stereotype or discipline a student?

We can break down the elements of relatedness into strategies that lead you and your students to engage this way.

Elements of Relatedness

Building relationships is a two-way street, but the teacher is the adult and a professional who comes with more communication tools, experience, and sense of self.

Please continue trying, even if a student doesn't seem particularly interested in getting to know you or in being known.

Besides the social, emotional, and academic reasons for fostering positive relationships, to do so is just good practice. Regardless of the academic impact, building positive teacher-student relationships is a valuable goal.

The following sections will explore why it's important to nurture relatedness with your students through positive teacher-student relationships, positive student-student relationships, and bias remediation.

Positive Teacher-Student Relationships

Building relatedness is the first step in helping your students learn and, as you will see, it has a dramatic impact on the other elements of student engagement. If relationship building is a priority in your classroom, it will open your students to the enhanced competence and autonomy-building strategies discussed in the previous two chapters. Academic self-concept builds in students who believe the teacher and classroom are comforting and supportive to their learning and growth (Martin, 2012). When students have not been successful at school, they have a critical need for a teacher to be what the great educator Rita Pierson (2013) calls their *champion*: "Every child deserves a champion, an adult who will never give up on them, who understands the power of connection, and insists that they become the best that they can possibly be."

The following effects can't be overstated.

- Relationships are a major source of people's personal happiness and a buffer from the stresses of life. Relationship loss is distressing (Argyle, 1999; Bronfenbrenner, 1974; Cowen & Work, 1988; Gaede, 1985; Glover, Burns, Butler, & Patten, 1998; McCarthy, Pretty, & Catano, 1990, as cited in Martin & Dowson, 2009).

- High relatedness increases *value of schooling*—when students feel that school is connected to their lives, useful, important, and relevant (Martin, 2003). This connection helps students develop significantly increased self-efficacy and higher engagement (Martin, 2007).

- High relatedness helps students function effectively in the school environment and internalize some of the teacher's beliefs about the content (Wentzel, 1999, as cited in Martin & Dowson, 2009).

- Socioemotional support leads to students' believing that they can succeed in class and valuing the subject matter more (Goodenow, 1993, as cited in Martin & Dowson, 2009). When they feel this acceptance from teachers, students engage more in class (Connell & Wellborn, 1991, as cited in Martin & Dowson, 2009; Niemiec & Ryan, 2009; Ryan & Deci, 2000), which could be one reason relatedness positively correlates with student achievement (Rolland, 2012).

- Classroom environments high in relatedness have a sense of trust and community (Mangiante, 2011), which are essential to learning, since students have to feel comfortable making mistakes.

You have certainly experienced this. When a student positively relates to you, the classwork and the course can become a favorite. The opposite is also true.

Failure to build positive relationships in the classroom leads to the following negative significant academic and social consequences (Martin & Dowson, 2009).

- Students who've had negative experiences can have negative academic self-concept, developed over years of feeling unconnected (Furrer et al., 2014).

- Students who do not relate positively to their teachers or classmates often turn to rebellion—being tardy, unprepared, rude, or unresponsive, for example (Skinner, Kindermann, Connell, & Wellborn, 2009, as cited in Furrer et al., 2014). Remember that these students are responding to a specific environment, and that they may have a totally different academic self-concept in another class.

- Students who feel disliked or rejected are, obviously, less likely to adopt the teacher's and classroom's cultures (Niemiec & Ryan, 2009, as cited in Jamison, 2014).

- Disaffected students have also been found to have strong sensitivity to a classroom's emotional tone (Schilling, 2009). If that tone is not nurturing and supportive, these students will never engage.

Disengaged students need to feel respected (Schussler, 2009). When we respect someone, we spend thoughtful time with him or her. We listen, and we try to understand. When you have felt disrespected by someone, that person was probably not trying to see your point of view. If a teacher does not show respect for the student's potential, the student cannot build the necessary relationship. Your behaviors must indicate that you have positive feelings about each of your students. Bear in mind that forming relationships is a marathon, not a sprint. Teachers can't give up because a student is, at first, not receptive or if there is a blow-up along the way. With some students, it is two steps forward, one step back.

When you consider how to meet students' needs, first think about their personal histories and how they perceive situations (Ng et al., 2018). Can you relate to their experience? These considerations impact your next steps. Your underperforming students, no matter their demographic, need you to build a relationship with them as part of a total intervention. It should be the *first* intervention for your students who have the most critical needs (McNeece, 2019).

Positive Student-Student Relationships

It's important for students to relate well to one another. These relations promote their engagement and academic achievement (Mikami, Ruzek, Hafen, Gregory, & Allen, 2017). The dynamics change as students age, too, showing "decreased academic motivation and increased receptivity to peer influence. Whatever the causes, the subculture of the peer group can be very telling in determining students' motivation to succeed in academics" (StateUniversity.com, n.d.). Like it does with competence and autonomy, classroom cultures that include cooperative learning play an important part in relatedness (Martin & Dowson, 2009; National Survey of Student Engagement, 2006). A cooperative structure gives students opportunities to make mutual goals and asks them to work toward those goals by sharing their intellectual resources (Martin & Dowson, 2009). It creates relatedness supports for all the students in your classroom.

Hostility or rejection from peers erodes a student's sense of belonging and academic performance (Furrer et al., 2014). Cooperative learning works against bullying. Start using the strategy early in the year, and use it often; it grows trust, togetherness, and belonging (Barkaoui et al., 2015). You can play many of the activities or games in this chapter throughout the year, but they can jumpstart a classroom's connectedness if used in the beginning of a school year. Use them as getting-to-know-you games in classrooms of all levels. Providing students with opportunities to talk about themselves is an excellent way to build a sense of student-to-teacher and student-to-student relatedness (Furrer et al., 2014; Marzano, 2007). Also, make sure to share *your* stories and interests with the students. A teacher who opens up is modeling. Students will adopt the norms you set, so show them openness.

Bias Remediation

What stops us from connecting with each student? The answer to this question is complicated and includes issues of proximity, time, and people, but one thing is clear: bias is the enemy of relatedness development (Cheng, n.d.; de Boer, Bosker, & Van der Werf, 2010; Urhahne, 2015). *Bias* is a preconceived notion about a person or group of people, and everyone has biases—conscious and unconscious.

What biases do you bring to the classroom? Being aware of one's own is a key to reducing or eliminating negative impacts (Gladwell, 2005). For example, assume a teacher has a student who doesn't do well academically and is angry and disruptive. Two years later, that teacher has that student's sibling in class. The teacher will be biased, even if unconsciously. If the teacher, based on experience with the older sibling, doesn't expect the younger one to do well academically, that actually affects the younger sibling's academic performance (Schaps, 2005; Urhahne, 2015).

It would also be foolish to think that thoughts about race, money, religion, or other social variables do not enter into the classroom. The ill of society will be the ill of the classroom (Muhammad, 2009, 2018). Remember, engagement and achievement are connected. Without relatedness, there is no engagement *or* fulfilled academic potential. All educators should focus on building relationships with all students while simultaneously recognizing the critical importance these relationships have for underserved populations. Those students tend not to feel connected and are most likely to disengage, experience academic fallout from that, and suffer from the consequences of that as students and as adults. When breaking down relatedness levels, researchers find that African American elementary students were more likely to say they have a negative relationship with their teachers (Wu, Hughes, & Kwok, 2010). The same study also finds boys are more likely than girls to say they have negative relationships with their teachers (Wu et al., 2010).

Consider the questions authors Lauren Porosoff and Jonathan Weinstein (2020) urge educators to ask themselves:

> Cultural biases define our notions of good behavior. For example, do we expect higher levels of self-awareness and social awareness from girls than boys? Do we honor the ways students with disabilities manage themselves and navigate social groups? When we imagine someone who makes responsible decisions, what kinds of decisions does that person make, what life and career path does that person end up having, and what color skin does that person have? When we look at the kinds of jobs a responsible decision maker might aspire to, what do the racial demographics in those positions look like? We might say we don't have these biases, but what do our special needs referrals and discipline records say? What stories do our grades tell? Which students' names do we hear, and in what contexts? Whose names are missing from our discussions? (p. 7)

Who is disengaged in your school? Do they fit a specific demographic? Is that demographic different than the majority culture of the teachers? A teacher's predeterminations—unconscious or conscious—about a student's potential impact learning outcomes (Muhammad, 2009, 2018), and bias often presents itself in subtle ways, such as when teachers pay less attention to a student, seat him or her farther away from the teacher's desk, and make less eye contact (Marzano, 2007). Be aware that favoritism is another form of bias. Favoring any one student can look like calling on one or a certain kind of student excessively, praising him or her more often, or allowing exceptions, such as a deadline extension (Martin & Dowson, 2009).

The reciprocal nature of relatedness is different than that of competence and autonomy. Teachers can also experience a negative impact from poor social interactions with students (Hastie & Siedentop, 2006, as cited in Van den Berghe, Cardon, Tallir, Kirk, & Haerens, 2016). What happens when you are called a name or a student hurts your feelings? What bias might you have toward students who haven't treated you well? Is it fair to let them fail? Would it be their fault if they did fail?

A learning-oriented teacher feels negative toward certain students at times, but separates those feelings from work, and does not allow the feelings to inform interactions with students. You might feel like rebellious students call your own competence into question. Disaffected students will not recognize or care that doing this is a problem (Furrer et al., 2014). In this kind of scenario, teachers might blame students for the problem. Let's recognize our ability to change the situation through our own actions. If you want to influence those students who are inciting negative feelings and inhibiting their own success, consider some basic rules from Dale Carnegie (1937) about always keeping interactions personally neutral to positive, because negative interactions will not help prevent a continued downward relationship spiral.

Confronting bias is critical per the evidence in the following list.

- When teachers were told to seek out misbehavior in a videotaped classroom, they spent much more time viewing the African American students (Gilliam, Maupin, Reyes, Accavitti, & Shic, 2016).

- After hearing a short verbal vignette about students acting out, different groups of teachers were asked what level of discipline the students should receive. The vignette across groups was the same— only the names were different. When the students in the vignette had traditional African American names, teachers recommended harsher discipline (Gilliam et al., 2016).

- African American and Latino students can be impacted by implicit bias they may have about their own abilities in school (Steele & Cohn-Vargas, 2013).

- Identity-safe classrooms, where students "believe their identity is an asset" and "are welcomed, supported, and valued whatever their background," produce higher achievement (Steele & Cohn-Vargas, 2013, p. 5).

Understand that every word you speak can either put you on a path to healing or a deeper disaffection. Instead of viewing negative student interactions as just a problem, teachers can view them as opportunities to gain information that can help them diagnose root causes for these interactions, and through identifying the causes they can reshape their responses to students (Furrer et al., 2014).

Relatedness-Building Strategies

Building a classroom culture of relatedness begins with the teacher—you. Your actions are a model for students, establish the norm, and build (or bruise) relationships between you and them. The activities you build in impact how your students relate to each other, also. When caring for others becomes a centerpiece in your classroom, relatedness, self-concept, and academic achievement increase. This chapter contains my favorite research-based strategies to accomplish relatedness. The following sections are split into positive teacher-student relationships, positive student-student relationships, and bias remediation strategies.

SCHOOLWIDE RELATEDNESS SUPPORT

Teachers demonstrate cultural competence when they consistently engage in positive interactions with their students, the parents of their students, and with one another. To help with that competence, consider implementing professional development opportunities. Formally training faculty about unconscious bias reduces its impact (Carnes et al., 2012).

What work does the school need to do to address unconscious biases? What kinds of programming and intervention can you implement to address bias remediation and build teacher-student and student-student relatedness in your school? Curriculum is one of the first places to look (and this meshes in some parts with relevance, which is discussed in the following chapter). Both teacher and students report—even in schools with majority populations of minority students—that curricula do not reflect the students' home cultures (Smith, 2019).

Integrating home culture norms into the school day is an effective strategy to help students relate with school (Muhammad & Hollie, 2012). Once the student sees the home culture, including home language, is a part of classroom culture, that increases relatedness.

Consider also the ratio of teacher ethnicity in your school. Studies show that race can be part of student achievement connected to teacher-student relationships (Dee, 2004; Miller, 2018), and far more white teachers than Latinx and African American teachers are in classrooms when compared to student demographics (Musu, 2019). It's as simple as this: "Students tend to be inspired by role models they can relate to" (Miller, 2018).

Ensure the following are in your school's hallways and common areas so students feel closer to their school as a whole.

- Display flags from all of your students', their parents', and their ancestors' countries.
- Display examples of students' home language, and have content-specific reading materials in the classrooms, library, and media center.
- In your office, display colors or prints that represent students' home cultures.

As a buildingwide intervention, it is a good idea to make sure at least one Tier 1, whole-building school improvement intervention strategy reflects that thinking. If you need intervention concepts, many of the instructional strategies in this book target students experiencing an achievement gap. For further study, I suggest *The Will to Lead, the Skill to Teach: Transforming Schools at Every Level* (Muhammed & Hollie, 2012), and *Overcoming the Achievement Gap Trap: Liberating Mindsets to Effect Change* (Muhammad, 2015).

Positive Teacher-Student Relationship-Building Strategies

How do we build positive relationships with students? Just like you would with any relationship, you'd be supportive and nurturing (Martin & Dowson, 2009). You would show empathy, care, and understanding (Cox & Williams, 2008; Furrer et al., 2014; Haerens et al., 2013; Skinner & Belmont, 1993, as cited in Van den Berghe et al., 2016).

Once you demonstrate curiosity about a student's life and share some about your own experiences, there is a connection. You develop empathy and, hopefully, the student does too. Reflecting on that student's experience and feeling empathy for him or her lead to caring about him or her. The actions a teacher takes based on a student's needs are acts of care. Like a doctor or nurse may treat a patient based on physical needs, teachers provide care for their students based on cognitive and affective needs.

Nonverbal Affirmations

Beyond what you say with your words, body language—nonverbal communication—speaks to your students (Marzano, 2007). The following list contains effective nonverbal strategies. How would you rank them from greatest impact on student achievement to lowest (Harris & Rosenthal, 2005)?

- Eye contact
- Gestures
- Smiles
- Physical praise (clapping, pointing, or fist pumping)
- Duration of interaction
- Frequency of interaction

To be clear, all of these strategies are effective, but which ones are most effective for you and why? Is there one you have not thought about trying before? Go ahead and try it. Additionally, remember to be empathic to students with developmental, emotional, or cognitive issues. Students will not always be able or willing to implement effective nonverbal communication; the teacher must set and maintain the model behavior. Your addition of more positive interpersonal interactions will make it more common for students to demonstrate the same behaviors. While you may have had varying success with the strategies in the preceding list, and your success with one strategy or another may be linked to your unique personality or skills, here is a ranked list of these six strategies' impacts based on research. Effectiveness is ranked from greatest impact on student achievement to lowest impact: (1) duration of interaction, (2) physical praise, (3) gestures, (4) smiles, (5) frequency of interaction, and (6) eye contact (Harris & Rosenthal, 1985, as cited in Marzano, 2007). These teacher behaviors help create the warmth that fosters connection (Furrer et al., 2014; Van den Berghe et al., 2016). Table 4.1 offers examples of opportunities for positive interactions with students, as well as those to avoid.

It might be difficult to avoid these negative behaviors when interacting with rebellious students or even when you're tired or hungry. Avoid the negative interactions at all costs; they are likely to make a student think, "That teacher doesn't like me," or "That teacher is so mean" (Furrer et al., 2014). When you make a mistake, apologize.

Apologies When Appropriate

Educators are not perfect, and the expectation that they should be isn't realistic. We all slip up sometimes; it is human nature. When we make a mistake that hurts someone's feelings and harms a relationship, we should acknowledge it and apologize. In the following, counselor Melissa Scott (2018) explains why apologies matter:

- Apologizing . . . re-establishes that you know what the "rules" are, and you agree that they should be upheld. This allows others to feel safe knowing you agree that hurtful behavior isn't OK.

- Apologies re-establish dignity for those you hurt. Letting the injured party know that you know it was your fault, not theirs, helps them feel better, and it helps them save face.

- Apologizing helps repair relationships by getting people talking again, and makes them feel comfortable with each other again.

Let's recognize how powerful our connections with students are. For example, the level of teacher-student relatedness reported by elementary students predicts how much engagement teachers observe in those students years later (Jamison, 2014). What we say and do today impacts the now and the future.

TABLE 4.1: Relatedness Behaviors

Positive Interactions	Negative Interactions
• Friendly verbal exchanges such as greeting students with a smile and a handshake at your door, going back and forth during clean-up or transition times, and saying goodbye at the end of the day • Interacting with a student whenever he or she initiates it (as well as you're able) even when it is not the best time. Hallway monitoring is an example of when you have a responsibility but the opportunity to learn a little about a student. Those who reach out might *need* to talk. If you can't talk with them right then, meet during a cooperative activity, after class, or during lunch. • Including everyone in classroom activities by rotating to ensure all students are selected • Remembering a student's name and using it during positive and neutral moments (versus only when he or she is off task, for instance) • Being aware of and acting in accordance with the student's background such as not asking about a holiday like Christmas with a student of a different religion or being sensitive about academic content when it might include characters or experiences that could make a student feel disconnected or even alienated from the classroom	• Verbally cutting off a student • Using an irritated tone of voice • Being sarcastic • Criticizing a student's abilities or personality • Rolling your eyes or sighing

Source: Furrer et al., 2014; Van den Berghe et al., 2016.

Buildingwide or Gradewide Relatedness-Building Events

As you have seen, students tend to become less engaged as they get into middle and high school (Jamison, 2014). This is probably consistent with many teachers' observations and maybe even your experiences as a student. Interestingly, the same study reports that when those same students report high relatedness in high school, they stay engaged (Jamison, 2014). However, building positive teacher-student relationships can be tougher at the secondary level, especially with students who have not experienced high relatedness at earlier grade levels.

Additionally, sometimes teachers at the secondary level refrain from expressions of warmth because they believe such expressions may be inappropriate for secondary-school students. For one small example, think of what a big deal Valentine's Day is in some elementary schools. It is common for teachers to create or buy valentines for their class, and the students for one another. The students find it fun, and exchanging valentines produces a positive feeling. Some secondary teachers and administrators believe it is childish or inappropriate to celebrate Valentine's Day this way with older students. Again, this is one example from my experience. What large-scale relatedness-building events does your own secondary school have? I'm not saying that high schools should celebrate Valentine's Day—it may, in fact, feel too childish—but secondary schools would do well to develop age-appropriate relationship-building activities that are all-inclusive and come without the social hierarchy common in secondary school.

One example of a way to celebrate with students that is appropriate for all ages is welcoming back students from breaks in an especially warm or fun way. At Avondale High School in Auburn Hills, Michigan (Benson, n.d.), and at Pinckney High School in Pinckney, Michigan, for instance, they have assemblies with music, presentations, and activities (Maurer, n.d.).

Your Experiences Shared

Consider sharing little pieces of your classroom-appropriate life experience with your students. Teachers say showing their human side is important for building relationships with students (Barkaoui et al., 2015), and research supports this: a teacher's self-disclosure leads to higher student motivation (Cayanus & Martin, 2008; Cayanus, Martin, & Goodboy, 2009). Vulnerability and self-disclosure help build relationships.

I used to tell my students about the family vacations I took to national parks. Many of my students had never been camping. I remember one time in particular when I was talking to my class about camping on a small archipelago on a large lake in Canada. A black bear came to the shores of one of our neighboring islands and watched us cook dinner. As dusk came, we canoed with the food packs to the third island and hung them in the trees. We waited before going back, listening for the bear to cross over to inspect our campsite or the other island. The students in my class would give me the collective, "Oh, no way. You're crazy," and I hoped they understood the message that wildlife is to be respected but not feared.

Every year with her high school classes, my wife shares stories about her challenges growing up as a kid in Alaska. She shares a deeply personal story about moving out of her parents' home at sixteen. After talking about the experience of leaving home and making it on her own, countless students have confided in her about their life challenges (M. McNeece, personal communication, September 25, 2019).

Do you share stories, especially from when you were a student yourself? Have you shared the exciting or important lessons you have learned, and even been able to connect them to classroom content? Let them know the joys or hardships you have overcome, because they have hardships too (Barkaoui et al., 2015). Talk to them and listen for their goals and interests while expressing unconditional regard for their development (Furrer et al., 2014). Students need to know their teachers are in their corner no matter what—that educators are their champions (Pierson, 2013). When you communicate that type of dedication to their future, students listen. This is how you create an accepting culture.

Of course, what you share will depend on students' ages, backgrounds, and maturity levels, the context, and other variables.

Opening up to your students is key. Just like with my wife's students, it can help them open up to you, and by being open, perhaps be better equipped to confront challenges in productive ways. The National Survey of Student Engagement (2013) suggests teachers ask themselves the following questions.

- "Have I talked to any students about their career plans?"
- "Have I worked with any students on something other than class content (such as committees)?"
- "Have I talked with students about our class 'topics, ideas, or concepts' outside of class?"

The questions are phrased so that the teacher takes initiative, but a student talking to a teacher about these topics indicates he or she feels safe enough to discuss them. That's vulnerability.

Positive Student-Student Relationship-Building Strategies

The following collaborative games develop a sense of comradery between classmates (and between the class and the teacher). Classrooms need to develop community, and teachers need to communicate that everyone is devoted to the group's well-being (Marzano, 2007). In a team atmosphere, students gain a sense of emotional support, and they share learning experiences, respect, care, and belonging with their classmates (Furrer et al., 2014). The National Survey of Student Engagement (2013) claims collaborative work between students is a leading engagement indicator. By developing positive relationships with fellow students, students are able to connect with their peers in a different type of social context, in which they understand new values and beliefs about learning (Jamison, 2014). In short, this develops your classroom's relatedness.

These kinds of peer relationships make the learning deeper and lead to newly positive academic self-concepts. I learned many of the following techniques from Ted "Milty" Miltenberger, former American School of Paris theater instructor, who was a guest professor of a master's-level class at Michigan State University where I was a graduate student. Ted left a lasting impression on me, and the games he taught with colleague Georges Duquette in my 1995 Laboratory and Field Experiences in Curriculum, Teaching, and Schooling: Ensemble Theatre Techniques in the Classroom at Michigan State University (and that Miltenberger cowrote about with Hana Svab [1995] in *Second Language Practice: Classroom Strategies for Developing Communicative Competence*) changed my classroom practice. These were the common games I used with my classes to help build relatedness.

The following relatedness-building games are effective for all grade levels and subject areas. You can adapt each one, and visit **go.SolutionTree.com/instruction** for additional strategies.

I Want to Know Someone Who

This is a great game to start the year. Students walk into the classroom feeling both excited and nervous about the new year, and this activity helps them get to know who has common interests or understandings. The following five steps will help you carry out this icebreaker, which you, the teacher, must play too.

1. Push the desks or chairs into a circle around the room with enough space for students to get into and out of each desk.

2. Have every student begin by sitting at a desk (or on a chair). Stand in the middle of the room and give the directions, say something about yourself, and change places with one of the seated students. The game is off and running!

3. Ask the student who is now in the middle to say, "I want to know someone who . . ." and add something he or she likes to do, play, learn, or have. It is up to the students what they choose. Some examples follow, if they need help getting started.

   - I want to know someone who likes playing football.
   - I want to know someone who loves sushi.
   - I want to know someone who plays volleyball.
   - I want to know someone who has a baseball card collection.
   - I want to know someone who is in Scouts.

4. Announce that any student who shares the sentiment should move to another desk—but not one directly to the left or right of the one they're currently in.

5. The person in the middle (in addition to the teacher who starts the game) quickly takes one of the empty desks.

The student who likes playing football is able to see the other students in the class who also like playing football. The student who likes sushi sees the other students in the class who do too. This lets us all know how similar we are, and it gives students an understanding of classmates with whom they may be able to begin a friendship. It also lets them get to know the teacher quickly and see that they even share some similar tastes in food, music, sports, and hobbies.

You may want to mention not running over people, and ask people to take it slow when they move to a new desk. Also remind them that the worst thing about *not* getting a desk is that they can meet some new people. Students can play this game for an extended period of time. Consider also doing a follow-up activity where you ask students what they learned about their classmates.

The Human Knot

Students really like this physical activity. You can do this as a whole class or in groups of two to three. Believe it or not, your students will work together to untangle their arms while playing this game. Natural leaders start guiding others, and no one can opt out because they are stuck in this human web.

1. Ask students to stand in a circle, and then to extend their right hands and take someone else's right hand. They can't take the hand of the person to their right or left.

2. Have students take a different person's left hand. The class is now in one big knot.

3. Insist that students untangle the knot without letting go of either hand. They must not put anyone in a position that makes that person feel uncomfortable.

    As they talk and work together to untangle the human knot, most times, they untangle into one big circle. Sometimes they untangle into an interlocked circle, which is also considered a solution.

4. After the group untangles, talk to them about what worked best and theories of action they could take as they enter the next round. Relate those group dynamics to the classroom, sports teams, and the workforce.

Team Counting

My classes love to play this simple team game when we're waiting for the bell to ring. The goal is to have everyone say one number and have the group finish; if you have thirty students, you have to make it to thirty. This works amazingly. The class can be silent for two minutes and, at the exact same moment, two people will say the same number. It's almost supernatural.

The following rules apply.

- While they're at their desks or in a circle, students number themselves, and the numbers aren't necessarily consecutive.

- You cannot talk unless you are calling out a number.

- If more than one student talks at a time, you have to start over.

- You cannot strategize, use nonverbals, or discuss who goes when.

- There is no time limit. You can wait as long as you want between different people saying a number. Students have to take turns using only their sense of whether another student is going to speak.

- You start over when more than one person at a time says a number, talks over someone, or numbers themselves incorrectly.

This is far more difficult than it seems because players start talking at the same time. It is almost eerie how we want to talk when we hear other people speak, and this game teaches us to listen to others. It also helps teach us patience. When a class finishes, they have a true sense of teamwork.

Coat the Room

This three-step game is physical and requires space because you're trying to coat the room entirely with evenly spaced students. I always use the example of spreading the butter evenly across a piece of toast. The toast is the floor, and the students are the butter.

1. Push desks or tables to the sides of the room.

2. Ask all students to bunch up in the middle of the room.

3. Say "Begin" (or play music or use some other indicator). Students move about the room with the purpose of everyone being exactly the same distance from each other.

   • They can talk and strategize (and even have to talk across the room to make sure everyone is unified).

   • They can ask the teacher if they've accomplished the task.

Obviously, the space and distance will always vary depending on your room and the number of students. This is a great time for you to move about and give feedback. The point is to get them to work effectively together. One person can't go rogue.

Eyes Down, Eyes Up

Have you ever met eyes with a stranger? What did it feel like? We spend so much of our lives avoiding eye contact with others. This three-step game helps us acknowledge each other and develop empathy (Atsushi Senju, as cited in Murphy, 2014).

1. Ask all students to form a circle with their heads down and eyes looking to the floor. Stand on the outside of the circle calling out directions.

2. Say "Eyes up" and have students look up and freeze while staring at someone's face. They can't stare off at the wall or window or floor. When two people's eyes meet, both students have to sit down (though you will have explained that sitting isn't bad; it just progresses the game).

3. After saying "Eyes down," have students look back at the floor. Repeat this until just one or two students are left. Games go quickly, so students who are out get back in right away. You are the referee if one person sits but the other doesn't because of a dispute about who locked eyes. Just keep the game going.

My students wanted to play this every day. They were intrigued by the connections they made. When we look people in the eyes, it makes them more human to us. When someone looks at you, he or she is recognizing you. If you ever have the chance to play the game, it is fascinating.

Cultural competency is always important, and this game is no exception. Eye contact has different connotations and rules in some cultures, and some students may have developmental reasons for struggling with eye contact.

Storyboard or Tableau

Think of this as a frozen game of charades in three parts—a human storyboard. This game makes clear the importance of facial expression and body placement when communicating. It works with all grade levels, but a short, simple story works best for elementary students.

1. Pair students or split them into groups of three or four. Each pair or group develops three freeze frames that tell a story.

2. After about five minutes, and once everyone has a section of the story, call a pair or group to the front of the room. The other students take their seats.

3. Have the audience close its eyes (or as Ted used to say, *close the curtain*). At the front of the class, the performing students arrange themselves for the first frame.

4. When the performers are ready, have the audience open its eyes and take in the first frozen scene for just a few seconds.

5. Ask the audience to close its eyes while the performers arrange themselves for the second frame.

6. Have the audience open its eyes again to take in the second scene for a few moments.

7. Do the same steps for the third frame.

8. Have the performers break out of their final freeze after a few seconds; they ask the audience to guess what story they told.

Mix up your groups to make sure all students are working with each other. You can also have students summarize a lesson or chapter from a book this way. It is an interesting way to check for comprehension. When starting this for the first time in class, model the activity.

Teachers and Students

This game builds creativity and makes students think about the words they are using. They will love seeing you participate here, too.

1. Pair students. One is the teacher, who gives the commands, and the other is the student, who does exactly what he or she is told—in a way.

2. The teacher role gives single-sentence commands, and the student role has time to complete a full action before the next command. The trick is that students try to twist the directions.

    Students must comply, but they are supposed to flip the command on its head. Think of how the book character Amelia Bedelia behaves. For example, when she is told to draw the drapes, Amelia pulls out a pencil and paper to sketch the drapes instead of pulling them closed (Parish, 1963).

3. After a few rounds of letting teachers and students switch roles, consider a classroom discussion about power, the multiple meanings in our English language, and creativity.

4. After the rounds, ask the students to share their favorite response.

Table Tennis

This two-step game is good for quickly bouncing ideas off other people.

1. Give the class a question, statement, or situation.

2. Students give multiple responses, going back and forth like a game of table tennis.

The first person ready goes first. The back and forth is less a competition and more about turn taking. An example could sound like this.

> *Teacher: The principal calls you down to the office. The first thing you say is . . . ?*
>
> *Student one: I didn't do it.*
>
> *Student two: I brought you this present.*
>
> *Student one: I was looking for the bathroom.*

It lets students explore all the reasons they may go down to the office and all the common things someone might say. Do not be afraid to use humorous situations. Letting students choose from a couple options, asking a different student each time you have a new prompt, or asking students to make up prompts allows autonomy at the same time.

Situation examples include the following.

- You greet a friend.
- Your parents said you can't borrow the car for the dance.
- Your girlfriend or boyfriend just broke up with you.
- You get home past curfew. What do you say?
- Your parent just found your room a mess. What do you say?
- You want the new video game. How do you ask for it?
- You want to ask out this one person. Where do you invite that person to go?
- Your grandma breaks wind in the car.

Sentence starters include the following.

- "You'll never believe it! I just . . . "
- "Today is the best day of my life because I just . . ."
- "The best way to say goodbye before winter break is . . . "

Students will be ready for a new starter about every twenty seconds, and after a few short rounds, it is time to move on. One of the main points of this game is to show students how similar their life experiences are. Because of that, make sure to mix the groups every so often. You can do this quick activity multiple times per week; you could make the last question activate prior knowledge necessary for the day's learning. As a special curriculum connection, consider using Table Tennis with English learners to help build everyday vocabulary (Duquette, 1995).

Chairs

This three-step game is my favorite because of what has manifested in the classroom when we play it.

1. Put two or three chairs in front of the classroom.
2. Set the scene by describing the situation and the characters who will sit in each chair.
3. Call on students to take on the roles. Students improvise the scene, but every so often, ask them to freeze so you can replace the actors with other students. The exchange focuses students on what is being said, because they may end up in the scene at any moment.

Exploring real-life situations increases their interest, as it becomes an opportunity for students to help each other process moments. To make a curriculum connection, use a scene from a book, a scientific discovery, or a historical event as a starter.

My class had a dramatic experience playing this game with a scene about a daughter wanting to be treated the same as her brother so she could go out with friends. The parents in the scene gave the same reasons for this biased treatment that my students heard in their actual homes. The girls in my class loved playing the roles of daughter, mother, older brother, and father. The improvisation revealed in these eighth-grade girls very intense and common feelings of a lack of fairness. Conversations continued after the scene, and many girls left with a bond that led to mutual support.

Card Scale

A deck of cards is a powerful tool in the classroom. It can promote thoughtful analysis by having the students create a mental model of levels or scales using the deck's order as a way to notice the difference. The cards can work as a scale for showing emotions, behaviors, and characters. I used a deck of cards in the beginning of the year to invite students to perform an emotion in a scenario like, *you just got an F on a test you studied really hard for*; sometimes it was two students discussing a topic. Both can get a secret card and have the debate (or agree) and then guess how different his or her partner's card was. The audience also gets to guess and scale in these games. For example, two students talk about having phones at school or how fun recess is. The teacher describes the scales and then deals a secret card to each. They have to discuss or argue based on their card scale. The class and the participants then guess the cards.

Other times it can be a charades-like game like the one Anthony and his classmates were playing at the beginning of this chapter. Play the game by using the following five steps.

1. Start with a term like *excited* and build vocabulary around that term. Ask questions like, "What is the opposite of excitement?" (dread) and "What is the center point between excited and dreading?" (neutral). The number two card would be dread, and the ace would be excitement.

2. Deal one card apiece to three students, who then leave the room.

3. Ask the students with cards to take turns coming into the room and acting.

4. The other students watch and vote on the number they think students are portraying. Before they vote, you can ask the class questions such

as "Was the character at a four or at a ten? Where would *you* be if you found out that (mention the given scenario) had just happened?"

5.   The performer reveals the card after students vote.

This is a nuanced way to describe emotional states or situations, and you could do this for almost any feeling or emotion students can explain. In my experience, acting and stepping out of comfort zones, while having the performance be part of the lesson, helps a student feel accepted. It also easily translates into discussions about how we feel.

This also makes for interesting ways to talk about characters in a book or a student's story. When you practice this card scale in your class with the student performances, it can become a common language to scale just about anything: "I think you wrote this character at an anger level ten, but based on what happened to her in the story, could you dial that up to a queen?" or "Romeo's anger is at a level three at the start of the scene, but then he gets to a ten and goes back down to a one—but by the end he is at a full-blown ace!" The cards work to deescalate a situation or help students understand an appropriate noise level: "You all are at a king right now. Can you collaborate around a level seven for me?"

This common language is an artifact of relatedness culture—a shorthand you all understand. It will help bond you together while also giving you a powerful tool to help students scale any nuance.

Bias Remediation Strategies

Bias remediation relies on being as objective as possible. For a scientifically objective perspective on your existing bias, you can take Harvard University's Project Implicit (https://implicit.harvard.edu/implicit) quizzes.

Bias in schools must be dealt with in three distinct ways: (1) adopting strategies to identify when bias is happening, (2) actively working to identify what bias is and where it may exist in the classroom, and (3) choosing new behaviors (such as changing "how you react to challenging behaviors;" Spiegel, 2012).

Addressing Bias

We can't address bias until we're aware of it. Research reveals, in various ways, that "becoming more aware of our biases can help us improve our interactions with others, decrease our sense of unease in interracial contexts, and make better decisions" (Suttie, 2016). Addressing our own bias privately is crucial to remediation, but it isn't the only way to do this kind of work. Discussing it in class with students in an age-appropriate way is also very important. This helps all students relate to each other in a healthier, more equitable way.

Use the following ideas to remediate bias in yourself and in your classroom.

- Have conversations when you encounter negative stereotypes. Help students recognize and process messages that display these stereotypes (Steele & Cohn-Vargas, 2013). One way to start is by using *I* messages, such as those suggested by Teaching Tolerance (2014): "It makes me uncomfortable to hear people saying that families from the housing projects don't value education" (p. 20). Reading books that include storylines with bias or stereotyping is an excellent way to begin the discussions with elementary students; *Mrs. Katz and Tush* by Patricia Polacco (1994) is a good start, and Social Justice Books (https://socialjusticebooks.org/booklists/early-childhood) suggests others by category. (Visit **go.SolutionTree.com/instruction** for live links to the websites mentioned in this book.) Current events can help with middle and high school students. Choose three news stories from three different sources and have students look for any bias in each.

- For middle and high school students, develop events that point out the stereotyping we all do, like a lesson where you show various pictures of people and ask your students to describe them, only to reveal actual personal traits (Steele & Cohn-Vargas, 2013). Don't have students do this opening at first, and when you use it, consider having them write their answers anonymously and in private or simply think them and not share. It is a difficult lesson, but very necessary. When I work as a consultant, I tell participants that being uncomfortable and learning are better than not talking about these biases at all.

- Make sure the stories you share or the books your class reads have opportunities to learn about characters who recognize their bias. One of my favorite books is *The Autobiography of Malcolm X* (X & Haley, 1984). There, Malcolm X relays how his bias develops and, near the book's climax, how he transcended that bias. When choosing books for elementary students, consider using Social Justice Books (https://bit. ly/2jUigPi) to guide your choices.

- Help students interact with diverse groups of people (Suttie, 2016). Do the same in your own personal or professional life. Research shows that interacting with people from diverse groups can help decrease prejudice (Denson, 2009; Gurin, Dey, Hurtado, & Gurin, 2002; Pettigrew & Tropp, 2006). Even more interesting, people who work in diverse groups routinely score higher on creativity indexes (Schmidt et al., 2019). In a diverse classroom, do this by creating random groups. In a homogeneous classroom or school, find ways to collaborate outside school. That might include Skyping or creating a Google Hangout with another school—including those from other countries—for the cooperative work done during class.

Increasing Empathy

Hanging signs that embrace inclusivity and safety is one way to foster this belief (Scharf, 2014), but it is only the beginning. Building student empathy is the next step. Empathy is concern for another person's feeling. Why is empathy important? It reduces bias (Suttie, 2016). Also, students with empathy have better communication skills and academic achievement, and are less likely to show bullying or aggressive behavior (Jones, Weissbourd, Bouffard, Kahn, & Anderson, 2018).

The following actions will help build equity in students (Jones et al., 2018).

- **Teach:** Spend time in class discussing empathy and why it is important to us as humans. Use modeling or share your empathic behavior in your daily life.

- **Act:** Expand a student's knowledge about other people and their challenges. When you expand students' sphere of understanding, you are more likely to grow care for them. Consider the opposite in war or even political campaigns—opponents attempt to reduce the opposition and dehumanize each other.

- **Talk:** When you are talking about a tragedy or injustice in the school, community, nation, or world, have your students do something about it. Provide the chance to help people with a real-world problem-solving project. No matter the size and scope, service learning grows empathy and has positive learning outcomes, too (McNeece, 2019).

- **Listen:** As obvious as it sounds, helping students learn how to actively listen is beneficial. Actively listening is silent listening, clearing your mind's eye of other topics or personal feelings, and staying judgment free. Consider having students take turns listening to one another. Because everyone, including adults, has a hard time doing this, consider adding this to a portion of a staff or school-improvement meeting.

Empathy is important to building positive relationships (Lesley University, n.d.). More positive relationships foster the belief that your classroom is an identity-safe place (Steele & Cohn-Vargas, 2013). When students respect each other's journeys, they help each other on those journeys. Sadly, when unchecked bias against a group or type of person is part of a school's culture, the effects are painful. A classroom culture that fosters empathy is a lifetime gift to your students.

Summary

Developing a high sense of relatedness like Anthony and Mrs. Hector did helps your students engage in school, learn more deeply, and develop positive academic self-concepts. What we do and say in our classrooms matters. Reflecting on our biases can help us engage every student. Creating classroom cultures where students can build trust collaboratively is one of the easiest and fastest ways to help students relate to us and each other and value school. That can be a driving force for their improvement as it becomes part of their academic self-concepts. Positive student-student relationships increase relatedness to school and the classroom, and boost students' in-school support groups. A classroom culture that bonds students together empowers them to unite and equips them to connect better with the world.

Interestingly, relatedness is just too big to put into one chapter, and it does not stop with personal interactions; students need to relate to content also. That is explained as relevance in the following chapter.

Use the "Teacher Self-Assessment Rubric—Relatedness" reproducible (pages 104–105) to evaluate your classroom's relationship-building culture.

Teacher Self-Assessment Rubric—Relatedness

Use this rubric to identify the research-based strategies that you implement in your classroom and those that can help you in your classroom tomorrow.

	4—Exemplary	3—Meets Expectations	2—Developing Skills	1—Emerging Understanding
Positive Teacher-Student Relationships (pages 87–91)	• My classroom artifacts convey my empathy, care, and understanding. • It is evident that I am involved in students' lives. • Students reciprocate with me and work to identify with their classmates in a similar way.	• Artifacts convey empathy, care, and understanding. • It is evident that I am involved in students' lives.	• I try to connect with students about current topics.	• I have trouble generating or have stopped trying to generate positive relationships with students. • My nonverbal or verbal interactions are neutral or potentially harmful to my relationships with students.
Positive Student-Student Relationships (pages 92–100)	• I consistently use different cooperative learning activities. • I make trust, togetherness, and belonging a classroom norm. • You can see a team atmosphere reflected in student actions and classroom artifacts.	• I sometimes use different cooperative learning activities. • Cooperative time and frequency vary, but students understand the activities and their purpose.	• I use at least one cooperative activity during the week. • Students generally comply with cooperative activities but are not enthusiastic or don't understand their purpose.	• I avoid cooperative learning or activities.

page 1 of 2

| Bias Remediation (pages 100–103) | • I engage students in discussions about bias or negative stereotypes when encountered in class material or modern events.
• I display artifacts that encourage students' personal growth related to their own bias.
• I regularly create diverse groupings.
• I display artifacts that value and convey safety for all identities. | • I engage students in discussions about bias when it is encountered in the classroom or school.
• My lessons invite students' personal growth regarding their connection to other people.
• Students' actions show that they feel safe. | • Conversations about bias are topical or brief.
• The displayed artifacts are pretty homogenous. | • I do not watch for bias.
• Possible bias-creating or stereotyping material or artifacts are unintentionally displayed.
• I avoid discussions about identity. |

page 2 of 2

CHAPTER 5

RELEVANCE

"English is the coolest class ever," Tom thought as he watched the screen in the dark theater. The crowd, filled with teachers, other students, and their families, and even his own parents, laughed at the slapstick jokes he had written into the movie. Months before, Tom's English class had started a project where they learned about characters, story arcs, and storytelling. They dissected movies to learn how they were written, filmed, edited, and marketed. Everyone wrote a screenplay, but Tom's peers had selected his script to be made into this year's eighth-grade production.

He peeked around at the auditorium, which was packed. People smiled as they watched. When the movie ended and the credits rolled, thunderous applause filled the room. Mr. Clancy, Tom's English teacher, was standing near the doors as Tom approached and said to him, "All of your effort really paid off. That was an excellent script—maybe the best one yet."

Before he could reply, Tom's parents came up behind him. "That was great! I had no idea it was going to be like that," and "I guess all of those Three Stooges marathons finally paid off! Thank you, Mr. Clancy. We never did anything like this when I was in school."

Mr. Clancy smiled and shook Tom's father's hand, "Thank you. I just try to use their natural talents and interests." Mr. Clancy said to Tom, "You'll be ready for freshman English. Read books this summer. There are some really neat ones on famous scriptwriters. You can pick up a few things."

Tom smiled, "Thank you; I'll do that."

"We'll get to the library tomorrow," said Tom's father.

• • • • • • • • • • • • • • ♥ • • • • • • • • • • • • • •

How do we get students to connect to the content we are teaching? How do we hook students on what the class is learning? How do we connect the curriculum to students' interests? Tom's English class captivated him not because standards like using dialogue and plot events by themselves are captivating, but because they related to his interest in movies. How Mr. Clancy uses that interest to drive instruction makes all the difference. Tom sees the skills he is learning as valuable. They are pieces he uses to develop something he is motivated to learn. This is the value of schooling (Martin, 2003). It is an academic booster behavior that successful students possess, and when coupled with feelings of autonomy, competence, or relatedness, relevance has an additional booster impact.

Relevance is when students see content as "interesting or worth knowing" (Roberson, 2013) or they see how the content "meets their personal or professional needs, interests, and goals" (Keller, 1983, as cited in Hosek, n.d.). This relevance is crucial to engagement (Barkaoui et al., 2015). Communicating the value of what your students are learning and how the concepts connect to their life experiences and aspirations (Orkin et al., 2018) is the first step to connecting students to the content.

We can break down the elements of relevance into relevance-building strategies that lead you and your students to this kind of engagement.

Elements of Relevance

Have you ever lost sense of time when working on a project during the evening, only to look up and see it was well past bedtime? Developing a student's sense of content relevance promotes this kind of experience. Teachers have a great deal of control about whether students connect to a curriculum. How you launch or hook students on a lesson matters a great deal. Methods for content instruction can help students see the relevance of what they're learning. Further infusing lessons with topics that are highly interesting to students and with connections to those things that are interesting to them is an excellent way to build a culture of relevance in your classroom. Relevance's three elements are (1) content, (2) interest development, and (3) delivery.

- To connect to your students' interests, see the Student Interest Surveys section (Schussler, 2009; page 115).

- To build a relatedness to their content through instruction, see the Modeling section (Fisher & Frey, 2015; page 118).

- See the Lesson Launch Strategies section for multiple ways to dramatically introduce students to content to get them hooked (Fisher & Frey, 2015; McNeece, 2019; page 123).

The relevance-building strategies in this chapter focus on interest connection and lesson launch. Interest in curriculum and content is a natural motivator. It is what students want to talk about.

Interest Connection

The earliest educators tapped into students' interests when teaching. Plato directed us to use what "amuses" the mind when teaching (as cited in Ely, Ainley, & Pearce, 2013). Though federal or state standards may dictate the learning targets, you can take elements of a unit and bend them to meet students where they are, not only cognitively but affectively. What amuses your students? What are they talking about with each other? What are they most interested in? Those are questions to think about as you work with your curriculum.

When a teacher uses materials and activities that relate to students' interests, it increases student motivation and engagement (Barkaoui et al., 2015; Ely et al., 2013) and makes it far more likely they will learn (Marzano, 2007). It's important to connect what students are learning to their lives, but it's more important to move beyond that and connect it to what interests them.

A little research goes a long way. As you relate to students, incorporate cooperative learning, and use the student surveys discussed later in this chapter, you will find out what their interests and dreams are. Even if you miss the mark, students will see your effort and appreciate it. It means you care. On a practical level, using high-interest content keeps students working. After finishing an exhausting learning task, introducing interest-based material can reignite learning and fuel new energy (Ely et al., 2013).

Understanding the *process* that engages a student's interest is helpful. According to educational psychologist Suzanne Hidi and education researcher K. Ann Renninger (2006), interest development contains the following four phases.

1. Triggered situational interest
2. Maintained situational interest
3. Emerging individual interest
4. Well-developed individual interest

Figure 5.1 (page 110) is a graphic representation of this model. Consider Hidi and Renninger's (2006) four-phase model of interest as you plan units and activities. How do you develop, trigger, and sustain interest in your content? How do you support students through their exploration? Do you use multiple steps to help grab and maintain their interest?

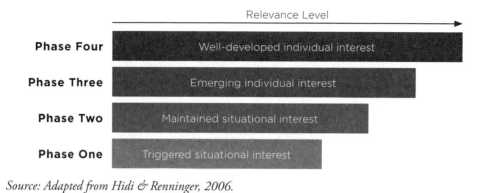

Source: Adapted from Hidi & Renninger, 2006.

FIGURE 5.1: The four-phase model of interest related to relevance.

Phase One: Triggered Situational Interest

This is how we introduce new material (covered in this chapter's Lesson Launch Strategies, page 123). Content that triggers interest might be characterized as surprising, incongruous, or intense (Hidi & Renninger, 2006). Students would be surprised if you transformed your classroom into a jungle; they would notice the incongruity of pairing a hip-hop song with personal finance; they would feel the intensity of having class in the pool for the first day of the unit on Melville's 1851/1967 *Moby-Dick*. The lesson launch strategies, such as introducing a mildly controversial subject, embody these characteristics. They tap into emotions, both positive and negative. It can seem counterintuitive to trigger student interest with something they might have strong negative feelings about, but it is effective. Just ask your students to write about a cafeteria food they don't like or about the dress code!

Sharing something about yourself might also pique students' interest (Frymier & Shulman, 1995). This approach, of course, also increases relatedness, because you are opening yourself to the students. For a secondary-level government class, talk about an experience that relates you to a historical event, like election night when you were a child. When teaching an elementary social studies unit about community, talk about how you and your neighbors interact. You have many life experiences on all sorts of topics—share those.

Phase Two: Maintained Situational Interest

When you've triggered and sustained situational interest, phase two occurs—an exploration of the topic where a student tries to find relevance to him- or herself (Hidi & Renninger, 2006). *Situational interest* is what students feel when they have just a spark of interest. This interest is still externally supported, and it can be fragile. How do you bring a class back on the second day of learning about a topic or skill?

Connecting back to the emotional trigger from the previous day is important. Cooperative group work is also a good option, since it can both trigger student interest in content and sustain exploration (Hidi & Renninger, 2006).

Nearly all the cooperative activities in this book are ready to spark interest. Sustained cooperative learning in the form of a card sort is an excellent way for a teacher using hip-hop to trigger students to gain interest in personal finance. The second phase (maybe on day one or two) could have a group card-matching activity where they connect lyrics with personal finance concepts. After the card sort, discussing personal finance concepts can lead into phase three of interest development: emerging individual interest. Examples from author Grant Sabatier (2019; https://millennialmoney.com/rappers-personal-finance) include lyrics from Notorious B.I.G., Jay-Z, and Drake.

Phase Three: Emerging Individual Interest

The third phase is characterized by a budding curiosity about the content the teacher has introduced (Abbott, 2017). Parallel to the concept of building a positive academic self-concept (chapter 1, page 7), this model's third phase has a student whose interest is triggered, has experienced a supported level of interest development, and has an emerging individual interest (Hidi & Renninger, 2006). At this point, the student is more resilient to setbacks and able to withstand misconceptions. Students are resilient simply because of how high their interest level is. This psychological development is akin to the development of a new academic self-concept, characterized by positive feelings about the content and knowledge, and students generally react favorably to reengaging with the tasks; they may even opt to participate by choice (Hidi & Renninger, 2006).

Have you seen a student get sparked, grow that because of a lesson, and attach personal interest to the content? Think of the hip-hop example. The teacher's next step is to help students apply personal finance to their lives and the lives of others. The students are ready to go more deeply in the topic, because it is relevant. Perhaps students could create a five-year personal financial plan as if they were an up-and-coming rapper.

Phase Four: Well-Developed Individual Interest

Phase four is when all the deep learning someone has done develops into an enduring interest, and students value the activity (Hidi & Renninger, 2006). The content that initially triggered the interest, and which the teacher nurtured, has become part of the student's positive academic self-concept. He or she values activities that include this topic or skill and looks forward to further exploration (Hidi & Renninger, 2006). Like the hip-hop personal finance lesson, a teacher has truly helped a student (who otherwise wouldn't have cared about a topic) see how it impacts him or her, work to comprehend it, and plan to transfer that information from the school to life outside. This is the goal—real-life topic relevance.

You could consider careers a specific kind of interest your students have. Developing career-relevant content helps engage high school students especially, who are notoriously difficult to engage (Orthner, Jones-Sanpei, Akis, & Rose, 2012, as cited in Abbot, 2017). School is about developing students' futures, so make sure that connection is explicit. What do they want to do when they are adults? This probably has a lot to do with your geographic area and with what jobs the adults in their lives have. If you know what careers your students are interested in, you can structure your interest development to match those interests. You can make sure the real-life problems that their favorite jobs solve are embedded in your content.

Lesson Launch

How you present content can act as the trigger for student interest. Be conscious of your communication when presenting material. Delivery matters. It should also be said that not all of us can be dynamic presenters. However, I have learned that there are some simple tricks to start with when developing your delivery.

It is essential to foster excitement and passion via your delivery (Barkaoui et al., 2015; Mangiante, 2011). The most student-interest-connected lesson or engaging teaching strategy will not be successful without your compelling delivery.

Remember, the student-teacher relationship is reciprocal. In my experience, when I had a flat day in the classroom, students were less engaged. A teacher's enthusiasm impacts students' effort (Schilling, 2009), and they can read us well. If your heart is not in what you are teaching, the students' enthusiasm will not be there either.

Fun matters. Do not be afraid to laugh with your students. Humor in the classroom is an effective learning strategy (Hackathorn, Garczynski, Blankmeyer, Tennial, & Solomon, 2011; Marzano, 2007), and it increases our relatedness (Hampes, 2009). Students will want to be there and work harder when the classroom is a fun place to be (Schilling, 2009).

Relevance-Building Strategies

Have you thought about your students' interests? Strategies can help you learn about students, build connections between interests and content, build connections between content and future careers, and hook students with dramatic, captivating lesson launches.

SCHOOLWIDE RELEVANCE SUPPORT

At the building level, deploy instructional rounds to focus on how staff build relevance. I define *instructional rounds* as when a teacher team decides to grow a practice or solve a problem with instruction. Then, one teacher opens his or her classroom to peer observation, so they can watch the practice everyone is trying to improve.

To accomplish instructional rounds, focus on a practice—in this case, how a teacher helps students see content as relevant in their lives. As the principal, identify teachers who are skilled at doing this and will volunteer to be observed. Ensure that all participants know that perfection is not possible and definitely not the point of instructional rounds. Even the act of opening a classroom to help colleagues learn should be commended.

To help facilitate growth around relevance and interest formation, observe a teacher for ten to twenty minutes (or maybe longer) near the beginning of a new unit. That way their ideas and the students' interactions and growth with those ideas are evident.

The team should establish behavior protocols prior to rounds. Those might include not interrupting the lesson, seeing how students interact with the concepts, taking notes about the strategies during the meeting, and agreeing on confidentiality about what everyone says during the meeting. The team leader facilitates a discussion about what worked well, what didn't, and why.

Most times, the administrator doesn't attend the rounds. Another teacher or an instructional coach usually leads the event. Also, instructional rounds are never part of the formal evaluation system. These rounds are about helping each other grow. Keep that a solid focus. After observation, thank the teacher who opened the room for the group. I like to create a poster and have the teachers who observed write, on a sticky note, something they saw that helped them grow instructionally. The poster is a thank-you artifact, and the notes recognize efforts. The teacher who opened her or his room should feel honored with process praise!

Interest Connection Strategies

Frymier and Shulman's (1995) relevance scale remains applicable (Fedesco, Kentner, & Natt, 2017). How often do you find yourself doing the following when you are trying to connect students to content by showing how it pertains to them?

- Using examples
- Providing explanations or activities
- Linking to other content

- Requiring students to apply content to interests
- Using current events

You can explicitly connect subjects and activities to those things you know students enjoy or talk about often in class. Ask middle or high school students what social media accounts they follow, including Instagram and YouTube. What do the people they follow talk about on their feeds? Table 5.1 links the things your elementary or secondary students might be interested in with different subjects. The secondary interests build on the elementary examples.

TABLE 5.1: Possible Interest Connections by Subject

Elementary Interest Connections	
Subject	**Interest**
Mathematics	Cooking, lining things up in rows, playing Minecraft or Tetris
Science	Picking flowers, collecting rocks, playing tag, swinging
English language arts	Singing, making up stories, role playing
History	Books set in different time periods, reenactments, museums
Physical education	Playing sports, leading games on the playground, making up games
Performing arts	Singing, dancing, pretending to play instruments, tapping in time
World language	Books set in different countries, eating at ethnic restaurants, listening to international music
Secondary Interest Connections	
Subject	**Interest**
Mathematics	Knitting, crocheting, sewing, sports, listening to music
Science	Bird watching, taking apart and customizing gadgets and computers, building model cars, bicycling, skateboarding
English language arts	Listening to or writing music, journaling, moviemaking
History	Movies, plays, or musicals about historical figures or events
Physical education	Playing sports, bicycling, skateboarding

| Performing arts | Creating YouTube videos, watching musicals, writing plays, playing an instrument |
| World language | Attending festivals, reading world news, traveling, volunteering at organizations that work with immigrant populations |

It's also important, especially for secondary students, to connect classroom content to their futures. Students want to grow and chase their dreams. Increasing relevance helps them see that what they are learning in your class can be a conduit to helping that happen.

Student Interest Surveys

Those who have disengaged and retreated (or who are introverted) most need you to learn, understand, and trigger their interests (McNeece, 2019). Students who are withdrawn from learning will be able to use a lesson based on their interests to reenter the educational environment (Schussler, 2009). Knowing student interests is the first step to connecting meaning to the curriculum (Orkin et al., 2018).

Ask students to fill out an interest survey a few times a year, since interests change and evolve. See figures 5.2 and 5.3 (pages 115–117) for surveys at two different grade levels. Also know that many of the questions for elementary students work for secondary students. Pick the best questions for your students.

Question	Answer
What is your favorite subject? What is fun about it?	
What is your favorite book? What makes it your favorite?	
What is your favorite movie or TV show?	
What is your favorite song or singer?	
What did you like learning best last year, either in school or at home?	

FIGURE 5.2: Elementary interest survey questions.   continued ⇨

Question	Answer
If you could choose one famous person, living or not, to be the substitute teacher for a day, who would it be?	
What do you enjoy doing when you're not in school?	
What three words describe you?	
What is one word that describes how you usually feel about school?	
What is one goal you have for the school year?	
What is something you would like to accomplish?	
What are you most excited about this school year?	
What else should I know about you?	

Source: Adapted from DePasquale, 2017.
Visit **go.SolutionTree.com/instruction** *for a free reproducible version of this figure.*

Question	Answer
What do you most look forward to when you wake up in the morning and why?	
What do you like to do in your free time and why?	
What is your favorite poem, short story, novel, or essay and why?	
When you think about life after graduating from high school or college, what career sounds good to you and why?	

What are three things you would like to learn this semester and why?	
Where would you like to go (to visit or live) after you graduate?	
What touches your heart?	
What do you want to change about yourself, this city, this country, or this world?	
What thing matters to you that doesn't seem to matter to other students?	

Source: Adapted from Ferlazzo, 2009.

FIGURE 5.3: Secondary interest survey questions.

*Visit **go.SolutionTree.com/instruction** for a free reproducible version of this figure.*

Advanced survey techniques may allow you to find out even more about students. There can be different ways to frame a survey so students are not retaking the same questionnaire multiple times a year.

Once you have the data, format them so you can use them. Consider doing the following.

- Developing an interest inventory data set to determine what interests students have in common

- Identifying local businesses, landmarks, or virtual field trips that may have connections to your students' interests

- Setting up experiences outside school or bringing in community partners and families as experts in various fields (Abbott, 2017)

Content

Building relevance to content can be as simple as building students' names and interests into the problems you have on an assignment or assessment—science, mathematics, and world languages are subjects where you can easily include students and the things they're interested in.

Building excitement about books is also important, especially for emerging readers. Use contemporary books with modern themes, allow a high level of autonomy regarding what everyone reads and what you read aloud, and ensure that students have time to talk about books with their classmates (Michigan Association of Intermediate School Administrators, 2017).

Modeling

Because students watch and mimic teachers, and hopefully adopt the classroom's behavior norms, modeling can trigger interest. When students saw me engaging in an activity, they could understand it as possible, enjoyable, or helpful. A teacher models by demonstrating and talking through decisions when solving a problem. Students use their own observations and the teacher's words to begin thinking about how *they* will solve problems.

Modeling with elementary students helps them develop problem-solving skills with both school work and social situations in class (Kelley, 2018). Additionally, students whose teachers model reading are far more likely to stay on task when doing sustained silent reading (Methe & Hintze, 2003). Finally, teacher modeling makes students more effective during the scientific inquiry process (Turcotte & Hamel, 2016).

Modeling has two key parts: (1) demonstration and (2) explanation in action (Fisher & Frey, 2015; Harbour, Evanovich, Sweigart, & Hughes, 2015). The demonstration includes showing students what they are preparing to accomplish. The explanation in action includes think-alouds about the difficult or confusing parts. This makes the new content less intimidating. When you're modeling, make sure to break your thinking and approach into parts or steps. For example, if I'm trying to get students to work an equation, after identifying or showing the equation in question, I talk through my initial thought about how to solve it and work the problem in front of students while simultaneously sharing my thinking, and saying what worked and what I thought was difficult. Both demonstration and explanation happen concurrently.

If you really want to pique interest, energetically model a bad example or an improper path to success and let yourself fail in front of the students. Students understand there is power in knowing what does not work! Make your thinking visible as you make these mistakes. It helps if you know the possible misconceptions that may arise when attempting to solve the problem. Let those misconceptions take you off track so students can learn from your mistakes.

As a middle school English teacher, I modeled the writing process for my class. I began writing a different story with each class. It was a generic story starter that began with a conflict and quickly included dialogue and gestures. I talked to students as I wrote, asking aloud questions like, "How can every word increase the thrill level, with the clock ticking and the walls closing in on the hero?" The students were really into the stories. A group of boys that had grown increasingly disengaged in class became really interested when I gave myself the same assignment I'd given them! After all, what kind of hypocrite would I be if I asked my students to write, but couldn't write myself?

I used contemporary themes and issues to hook students. From there, I modeled and talked aloud with them about the skills they were expected to have. I let students see how flawed I was as a writer. When we were reading a draft, they often found errors, and I gave them small bags of hot Cheetos as an editor's fee. They ate it up—literally. They saw me being honest about making mistakes instead of hiding or feeling embarrassed about them. Even tough boys wanted to write, because they saw how much fun it is to walk side by side through the process.

Their growing interest in writing and collaboration was a huge payoff, and the standardized exam results echoed that. My class had a passing rate of 92 percent on the state writing test. Even those who did not pass the exam showed growth, and two students went on to complete their own manuscripts from the stories they wrote that year.

Future Job Surveys

Future job surveys are popular. You can never develop a complete list of the jobs that will be available to students, but you can develop a simple checklist with an open-ended write-in option. Consider using a version of the surveys in figure 5.4 or figure 5.5 (page 120), or doing this in electronic form if you want data you can see in front of the class. And you don't have to administer a survey. You can ask students about their futures in an informal way. Ask them from what careers they would like professionals to speak to the class, for example.

Which of these careers interest you? Mark an X next to all that apply.		
Meteorologist	Business owner	Firefighter or police officer
FBI agent	Writer	Designer
Nurse or doctor	Environmentalist	Veterinarian
Dentist	Lawyer	Media developer
Engineer	Artist	Politician
Performer	Teacher or principal	Other:
Athletic trainer or coach	Computer expert	Other:
Chef	Military	Other:

Source: Abbott, 2017.

FIGURE 5.4: Career interest survey—elementary school.

*Visit **go.SolutionTree.com/instruction** for a free reproducible version of this figure.*

Which of these careers interest you? Mark an X next to all that apply. When asked to circle one of the options, please do so if you've marked an X next to it.		
Meteorology	Business ownership, business administration, or finance (circle one)	Firefighting, law enforcement, or FBI agent (circle one)
Agriculture, forestry, or conservation (circle one)	Marketing, public relations, or sales (circle one)	Fashion or interior design (circle one)
Dentistry, doctor, or nurse (circle one)	Health science, environmentalism, or research (circle one)	Veterinary science
Hospitality and tourism	Lawyer or judge	Digital or social media development
Architectural, electrical, civil, or technological engineering (circle one)	Professional painting, writing, music, or 3-D artistry (circle one)	Government, civil service, or politician (circle one)
Welding, mechanical, or machinery work (circle one)	Teacher, principal, or professor (circle one)	Other:
Athletic training or physical therapy (circle one)	Technological support or computer programming (circle one)	Other:
Chef	Military	Other:

Source: Adapted from Abbott, 2017; Hidi & Renninger, 2006.

FIGURE 5.5: Career interest survey—middle and high school.

*Visit **go.SolutionTree.com/instruction** for a free reproducible version of this figure.*

Consider having students provide an interest scale. Instead of just saying "I want to be a firefighter," have them reflect on each job's different responsibilities and rate how interested they are in each job. After they review all of those responsibilities, consider having the class compile a list of them so students can share their expertise. Make that information accessible to everyone, maybe in the form of displayed posters or class presentations, and share it. Consider choosing a few jobs that are common in your region, but always add jobs that expand the students' current worldviews.

Also, an important difference between these surveys and official future job surveys is the former are about both expanding what jobs students consider *and* providing information to you about your students' interests. Use these data to develop content that connects with the futures students see for themselves. These will help students see the connection between content and their interests. Visit **go.SolutionTree.com /instruction** for live links to careers related to specific topics, including world languages, physical education, and performing arts.

Extension

Students need extensions to develop a deeper interest. These are the activities that often we feel there is not enough time for. Without extension or enrichment, students can learn and master material, but they will not have a chance to move into the latter two phases of the four-phase model of interest building to grow a real passion for what you teach (Hidi & Renninger, 2006).

How can you support enrichment in your classroom? Educators and authors Lynn Geronemus Bigelman and Debra S. Peterson (2016) offer the following basic classroom examples.

- Have rigorous material for our students to study and research. In a younger mathematics class, this may be a real-life application of the mathematics concept like a bridge building kit or in a middle school English class having canonized text available for students to examine, like Shakespeare's complete works.

- Classroom learning should always allow for deeper and student-initiated study when their curiosity is piqued. If a student is really interested in World War II content, make sure you allow that student dedicated learning time to continue exploring his or her interests.

- As identified throughout the book, use cooperative activities or group work time where students can push each other's thinking.

The Movie Project (based on an experience I had as an eighth grader teacher) and The Douglas Show are two ways I extend learning for my students.

The Movie Project

The Movie Project was an after-school club I opened to all students at Levey Middle School, and the goal was to write, act, film, direct, edit, and present a student-made movie. Most students love movies. We started our work in the spring, when the marketing for the Hollywood summer blockbusters would begin hitting the radio and television stations. There was always a movie that the students would be excited to see. It made sense to use that enthusiasm to trigger their interest.

The story about Tom from the beginning of the chapter comes out of my experience as a teacher when doing this project. The project would end with a real movie between forty to sixty minutes long. We had an opening night celebration at a local movie theatre. There was a red carpet, photographs, and popcorn. The movie played in school to celebrate this presentation of combined language arts skills. It was for the eighth graders in their final semester of middle school.

There was a high level of collaboration. Teams worked together to make sure their movie was going to top the previous year's class. We downloaded modern movie scripts, learned to read lines, and familiarized ourselves with the structure of a Hollywood script, and then watched the films with the scripts in front of us so we could see how a script comes to life. We studied the masters and saw that they had the ability to recreate scripts around their own ideas.

Students usually do not recognize that movies start as ideas on paper. All students during this project worked on scripts, usually in pairs. The class read the scripts and ranked each one. Once they identified the best ones, students discussed what made them work, and the team took all the best to create a new, final script that brought in the best elements to make sure we had a winning film. This is how one year we had a movie that was a mix between Shakespeare's (1600, 1973) *Henry IV, Part 2*, and space-themed science fiction. The students' creativity was always the centerpiece.

The hard work and pride with which they applied their ELA skills transformed into an excellent presentation of student work. The community celebrated these works of art. Students designed huge movie posters, which we printed and hung on the walls, sparking the interest of younger students as they walked the hallways.

When I see students from one of those classes, that experience is the first thing they talk about. An ELA class transcended a traditional school framework and became a milestone in many people's lives, including my own.

The Douglas Show

The Douglas Show was a weekly newscast created by K–6 students at Douglas Elementary in Garden City, Michigan. It functioned as an intervention for students struggling with ELA, but neither the students nor the parents knew that. We integrated the ELA skills they needed to improve into the process of creating their newscast. The students' interest was triggered by the cool factor and the performance aspect. The newscasts had small segments totaling between fifteen and thirty minutes.

The news crew rotated on a weekly and monthly basis, and students did different segments each time. They would brainstorm, write, practice, and perform their segments—reporting news on our school, local and national events, cooking, and books. They also offered a vocabulary word of the week, weather forecast, and sports roundup. We filmed and edited the show to make it seem live but allowed for the necessary retries.

When students who did not need the intervention asked to be a part of the show, we had them independently create a different part of the newscast. Sometimes, teachers of different classes submitted commercials and news segments. On occasion, I filmed a brief segment with a class if they had a neat idea; that way, the intervention teacher could stay focused on the students who needed it the most. When the weekly Douglas Show aired on Friday afternoons, the whole school stopped and watched intently. The newscasters became the celebrities for a week. Where a student had struggled became the reason he or she was highlighted and celebrated. The Douglas Show changed academic self-concepts.

As the show's popularity grew, we began playing it over the school's cable station. We were asked to show it regularly at the school board meetings. Parents would tune in to watch their child's newscast. Members of the community, those without school-aged children, would call the school to tell us how neat it was. Over the summer, we reran all of the shows. Parents reported that students would seek it out to watch over and over on their own. Participants received recordings of their newscasts, which they shared with family members who lived far away.

The newscast extended students' learning. They were highly engaged and used their language and research skills while growing their interest in reporting or producing. They worked collaboratively and independently, but there was a team feel each week.

Lesson Launch Strategies

Let's face it, you can start a lesson one of two ways: in a traditional sit-and-get way or by grabbing the most interesting part of what students will learn and revealing it in style! If you trigger students' interest when you launch a lesson, you build relevance.

Launching learning was a concept introduced in Fisher and Frey's (2015) *Unstoppable Learning* and expanded on in my companion book, *Launching and Consolidating Unstoppable Learning* (McNeece, 2019). Fisher and Frey's (2015) Unstoppable Learning model includes launching and consolidating as distinct pieces of the relevance puzzle. *Launching* is the hook. *Consolidating* is the activities that take students through tasks. The energy and interest that you create when you launch learning can carry on throughout a lesson.

Author Dave Burgess (2012) is a master of instruction hooks. Making sure your delivery is engaging is the last part of the relatedness puzzle, and Burgess's (2012) following strategies, with examples from my experiences, are ones you can use tomorrow to increase relevance.

- **Kinesthetic:** Get your students to stand up and use their bodies and the new vocabulary words they are learning. For instance, a middle school social studies class stands up, each student holding a small sheet of paper with a single syllable on it. The new vocabulary words are on the board. Each student has to identify which word he or she belongs to and find the right word group. For example, the four students with the four parts of *am-bas-sa-dor* find one another. At the end, students say their syllables in order in front of the class.

- **New location:** Get your students outside of the classroom when introducing new material. Use your school's environment as a way to trigger interest. For example, the high school algebra class, rules in hand, goes to the school courtyard to find all the sloped lines they can. In inches, they document the rise and run of all these sloped lines.

- **Human props:** Use your class as props for the setting of the article or the story you are reading. A first-grade teacher is getting her students excited about a new story. She brings students up to the front of the class to be the characters of the new story and elements of the setting, like the doorway (two students standing, facing each other, with their hands on the arms of the other student).

- **Music:** Introduce new content by bringing in music from the time period or culture in which the content originates. YouTube has all the songs you will ever need, from chamber music to Billboard top hits. Imagine having the top tunes from 1965 playing when students come in for the first day of reading the book *The Outsiders* (Hinton, 1967).

- **Room transformation:** Decorate your room to connect with a theme you are teaching. For example, a mathematics teacher may alter the room by putting an X and Y plot on the floor with tape. The students use the floor tiles as units and are able to place and talk about the points. You can display data using this strategy and the human props together, where students are the points on a line or columns in a bar graph. A high school English teacher in my district has a Gatsby party each year, complete with a roaring twenties décor, costumes, makeup, and ginger ale.

- **Costumes:** There is nothing wrong with dressing up. Use a special outfit or actual costume to trigger interest. When her class was deciding what book they wanted to read next, an elementary teacher in Arkansas dressed as a chef, complete with white apron and hat, and the books were the entrée. The students watched short videos about each book and decided, like they do during competitive cooking shows, which books moved on. My favorite thing to do was dress up like a greaser on the first day of reading *The Outsiders* when I was a middle school ELA teacher. How does the main character in your class's current book dress?

Questions

What part of the lesson will be most dramatic? Pointing out novel information when you are connecting students to new learning is a very effective strategy (Marzano, 2007). For example, when a high school art teacher introduces a unit on Leonardo da Vinci, instead of starting with his humble beginnings, ask questions such as those that follow and project *Mona Lisa* on the wall.

- "What is the lady in the painting thinking?"
- "How much do you think this painting is worth?"
- "How many times do you think this painting was stolen?"

A little research can reveal some unusual details that will grab students.

Mild Controversy

Robert J. Marzano (2007) suggests creating a mild controversy. What controversy exists in the content that you are covering? From mathematics to art to physical education, if you do some research, you will find a controversy. (In fact, searching online for *hypotenuse controversy* reveals that Babylonians discovered the Pythagorean theorem hundreds of years before Pythagoras was credited with doing so; Ratner, 2009.) You can expand how you examine controversy, too. If you are interested in exploring a controversy born from, for example, a radical belief where people ignore facts based on contemporary research, search online for *flat earth society* to find people who don't believe the planet is a sphere! You can engage students in a discussion about what forms controversy can take. For instance, is some controversy more acceptable to the mainstream and why? Do people crave controversy or fear it; do we need it? How might one approach controversy as part of the learning process?

Video

Short video clips can trigger interest. Research videos and other media ahead of time. There is amazing content and examples of people doing outrageous things. From *physics tricks* to *epic wins* (steer clear of *epic fails*) to *math tricks* to *people are awesome*, consider launching your content with a clip that will spark interest in your subject area.

To flip things around, consider having students complete video presentations and watch those with the class. Students can seek interesting information about what you are going to learn. Student recall is best when learned via video-based experience (Nuthall, 1999; Nuthall & Alton-Lee, 1995). Flipping the launch not only triggers student interest but boosts autonomy.

Summary

Students who are highly interested in the topics you're teaching find relevance and value in what they are learning. A classroom culture that focuses on making learning interesting and content relevant helps build students' affective connection to school. Using the strategies in this chapter will help you achieve that engagement, which can lead to self-efficacy. Really push the limits. Doing that will help your students connect to the content like Tom did in the beginning of the chapter.

Use the "Teacher Self-Assessment Rubric—Relevance" reproducible to evaluate your classroom's relevance-building culture.

Teacher Self-Assessment Rubric—Relevance

Use this rubric to identify the research-based strategies that you implement in your classroom and those that can help you in your classroom tomorrow.

	4—Exemplary	3—Meets Expectations	2—Developing Skills	1—Emerging Understanding
Interest Connection (pages 113–121)	• In addition to meeting all criteria in level 3—Meets Expectations, I have a keen understanding of the content that will engage students and what will not. • I display high-interest artifacts, including modern topics. • I embed surveys in the lessons.	• I use surveys or other forms of student input to help determine content delivery. • My comments reflect a knowledge of student interests. • I consider student interests before starting every new lesson.	• I use surveys or inventories at the beginning of the year and use the results to connect to student interests. • I develop student interests topically, or I use those from previous years.	• I don't adjust the content to student interests.
Extension (pages 121–123)	• I support students so they can go deep in many different and creative capacities. • I display artifacts from students' previous projects. • I consistently give students time to go deeper or give them weekly or monthly specific time. • I structure lessons so students can go as deep as they are willing to go.	• Students have the regular option to go deep with their learning. • I mentor groups who are going deep.	• Lessons rarely allow students to go deep.	• I cannot allow students to go deep due to the tight instructional schedule.

page 1 of 2

Lesson Launch (pages 123–126)	• I use multiple delivery formats (questions, novelty, mild controversy). • I consistently deliver content creatively or in an out-of-the-box way.	• I launch learning for every new unit. • I consistently use different delivery methods for instruction.	• I make some attempt to engage students when I deliver content.	• It is difficult for students to stay attentive when I launch lessons.

CHAPTER 6

CULTURE CHANGE

The fact is that a spectrum of engagement exists in classrooms all over the world. Creating an engaging classroom full of students who feel competent, who enjoy autonomy, who relate well to the teacher and to one another, and who can see how content is relevant to their lives requires a focus on developing a classroom culture of engagement. We are the creators and keepers of that culture.

Culture has been a passion of mine since I read *Transforming School Culture: How to Overcome Staff Division* (Muhammad, 2009, 2018). This passion grew so large it became the focus of my doctoral dissertation. While engaging in my study, I came across some truths about what culture is, who creates it, and how it changes. The concepts of culture I learned about in academia mirrored what I saw in the classroom and school and deeply resonated with me. I saw the parallel between the literature and how a true esprit de corps was formed and nurtured. Understanding your impact on your classroom's culture is powerful. Explaining the concepts and providing tools and strategies to help you develop a classroom culture of engagement are my goals in this book. Let's go deeper into how understanding culture helps us develop this.

First, understanding how culture originates and develops matters. It is your understanding and powerful position that can change things. As you read through the previous chapters containing multiple strategies, you were hopefully thinking about the norms, values, and beliefs that fill out your classroom's culture. Because change is difficult, this chapter lays out the next steps. Changing a culture—how we do business in our classrooms—can be scary. You will learn this material, using the "Student Engagement Needs Inventory—Grades K–3" (page 142) or "Student Engagement Needs Inventory—Grades 4–12" (page 144; both adapted from a myriad of sources, including García-Ros et al., 2017; Green et al., 2006; Martin, 2007; Ng et al., 2018; Orkin et al., 2018; Parsons et al., 2014; Schilling, 2009; Snipes & Tran, 2017; Wang, Bergin, & Bergin, 2014) with your students, and finally, adopting the new practices that will engage your students. Your instructional risk taking is going to make a difference.

But first, how is culture defined, cultivated, and manifested?

How Is Culture Defined?

To explain more fully and to understand a teacher's impact and potential to adjust that cognitive and affective engagement, we have to first define culture. Culture is powerful and complicated. It is the unspoken social contracts that drive our decisions, even when we don't know they are doing so. Slightly different cultures, as small as your family and as big as the largest military organization, exist in every human group. They socialize us before we even comprehend their presence. At its core, culture is our underlying beliefs about life and living (Schein, 2010). Our beliefs help us make our plans, and our plans determine our actions. This is not norms or climate.

How Do We Cultivate Culture?

Culture develops in a few different ways (Schein, 2010).

- **The leader's beliefs, values, and assumptions:** The leader in this scenario is the teacher. The underlying beliefs include what you feel is most important. As you create new cultures, think about how you feel about yourself, your colleagues, and your students. What can you accomplish? Do you feel self-efficacious, autonomous, and competent? Do you value those things, and do you believe it's important for other people to possess them? What are your students capable of? Are they capable of handling autonomy? Are they competent and worth getting to know better? Does what they're learning mean something to them, and if it doesn't currently, can you help them see how it does?

- **The learning experiences of group members as they solve problems:** Problem solving is how groups evolve their cultures. During a day or a week, what problems do your students solve? In other words, does the work that you assign build a sense of competence? Does your instructional and behavioral approach build autonomy? When students work, is it collaboratively, to build relatedness? Are the problems related to the students' perspectives and the real world?

- **New members or leaders introducing new ideas:** Each start of a school year is a new group of people coming together with the teacher, who is the leader. The students bring their previous experiences and understandings about what learning is, but the teacher is the most powerful force for creating this new culture. Students who begin later in the year alter the culture, but they are also socialized by the class's established norms and usually pick up the expectations quickly.

How Is Culture Manifested?

Former MIT professor and guru of organizational culture Edgar H. Schein (2010) claims that the "only thing of real importance that leaders do is to create and manage culture" (as cited in Peterson & Deal, 2009, p. 17). Students will adopt the behaviors, values, and beliefs we consistently communicate and model. Harry K. Wong and Rosemary T. Wong's (2001) *The First Days of School: How to Be an Effective Teacher* instructs new teachers to establish these classroom routines and norms from the first minute students come into the classroom. This is not a coincidence. Wong and Wong (2001) are instructing new teachers to begin developing the culture.

Students aren't the only ones who show up with experiences influencing their beliefs about learning. You bring experience from past years to the new year's class. Watch for bias and know that challenges are not a bad thing; we just need to reflect and work on them. The biggest challenge that you address each year is how you will help your students grow from the beginning of the year to the end: *learning* is what your classroom culture will affect most.

Of course, every year there are new challenges. You've certainly had a lesson work well one year and bomb the next. Have you ever been on extended leave and returned to find that your students have learned a few behaviors (positive or negative)? That new classroom leader made a mark.

Schein (2010) asserts that culture manifests itself in three basic forms: (1) artifacts, (2) espoused values, and (3) underlying beliefs. You transfer underlying beliefs with your espoused values, and they manifest into artifacts. See figure 6.1 for a visual representation.

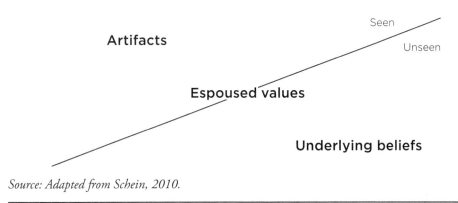

Source: Adapted from Schein, 2010.

FIGURE 6.1: Culture manifestation elements.

Artifacts

The first level of culture is artifacts. *Artifacts* are the things you put up in your room, including student work, and the observable behaviors—the norms of how you speak with your students and how your students speak to one another. An observer can walk into your room and see the artifact level of culture. What completed projects are on the walls? How are the students interacting? Is there silence, or is there the hum of industry? What are the stories you tell your students?

The instructional engagement rubrics at the end of chapters 2–5 ask you to look for specific artifacts or behavioral norms. You can see this manifestation, and you are empowered when you can look around your room and see what healthy classroom norms you've cultivated.

Espoused Values

Espoused values are what we devote time and energy to. Espoused values are the next level of culture, slightly deeper than the artifacts level. We cannot see these values, but they show up in our repeated actions, and in our artifacts. For example, the first letter you send home to parents and guardians is an artifact. Does it communicate what you value in the classroom? Do you review a list of rules and protocols for homework, or do you talk about your vision for their children's learning? Sometimes, we don't intend for the artifact to communicate the values it does. For example, if your school or classroom celebrates your positive behavior support program, that is an artifact that communicates the school values good behavior. What does your school do, on a monthly basis, to celebrate *learning*?

Underlying Beliefs

The final level of culture cannot be seen either. It manifests as the *underlying beliefs* that are within your school, classroom, students, and self. As the leader, your beliefs can become your students' beliefs. Students rise or fall to our expectations (Fisher et al., 2016; Hattie, 2012; Marzano, 2007). Do we believe that all students can be engaged and, most importantly, do we believe that *we* can engage them? Do we believe that all students can learn? The necessity of believing that all students can learn and engage is why it is critical to monitor your bias (page 83). It is unethical for any member of a school community to predetermine or anticipate failure for a single student (Muhammad, 2009, 2018).

Chapter 1 (page 7) explained academic self-concept—what a student believes about his or her ability to learn. If teachers build a culture of engagement by nurturing competence, autonomy, relatedness, and relevance, students will adopt the teacher's belief that all students can reach the highest of expectations.

This book describes the kinds of artifacts that you will find in a high cognitive, high affective classroom. What do your classroom's artifacts communicate about your values and beliefs? What do they say to parents and guardians, staff, administrators, and—most importantly—students? Can you see how the artifacts develop feelings of competence, autonomy, relatedness, and relevance? To help you see that evidence, complete the "Teacher Self-Reflection—Artifacts" reproducible (page 134).

As you complete the reflection, consider the following questions.

- What cooperative activities help students support each other (competence)?

- What norms do you have around student choice, and what items reflect that (autonomy)?

- What item or behavior conveys how connected you are to your students, and vice versa (relatedness)?

- What activities or items reflect how your classroom content is relevant to students' lives, now and beyond formal schooling (relevance)?

Summary

Students adopt the classroom culture of engagement built by the teacher. That culture reveals itself through artifacts, espoused values, and underlying beliefs. Luckily, teachers are classroom culture leaders, and knowing how to create culture and reflect desired values can help you engage students so they develop a true love for learning.

Teacher Self-Reflection—Artifacts

Follow these steps after reading the book and completing this reproducible.

1. Every teacher team member brings his or her completed reproducible to a designated team meeting.

2. The team creates one poster each for the engagement elements: one for competence, another for autonomy, another for relatedness, and another for relevance. Add to the posters what everyone wrote on their reflection. (You can use sticky notes, but there is no rule about having each teacher write on the poster.)

3. Once completed, conduct a gallery walk, where smaller groups rotate to each poster. Allow everyone ample time to talk about each separate element's poster. The information will help you share engagement ideas, and everyone will leave with new engagement tools.

4. Keep the posters and celebrate them as artifacts of your dedication to engaging all students.

Engagement element	Artifact (Behavior norm, language, story, displayed work, exemplar)	What belief or value does that artifact say about your classroom's culture of engagement?
Competence		
Autonomy		
Relatedness		
Relevance		

EPILOGUE
GOING FORWARD

In *The Art and Science of Teaching*, Marzano (2007) states that "No amount of further research will provide an airtight model of instruction. There are simply too many variations in the situation, types of content, and types of students" (p. 4). I believe this is true, but the mixture of competence, autonomy, relatedness, and relevance is the big bucket that every effective strategy fits into.

When teachers describe to me strategies that have worked with students, no matter what they were for, each strategy fits into the competence, autonomy, relatedness, or relevance components. Ask colleagues at your next team meeting about the strategies they use to engage their students, and you will also be able to categorize them into those components. No matter the subject or grade level you teach, the strategies I have shared offer the ingredients that students need. The learning environments that we create and the relationships we form are more powerful than a student's ability, ethnicity, or gender (Hattie, 2002). *Teachers* are the most influential part of an effective school (Marzano, 2007).

If we do nothing different, continuing out of fear or habit, students will not learn at higher levels. Once you gather information on the rubrics included in chapters 2–5, you will know the engagement impact you currently have on your students. Look back at the self-efficacy cycle in figure 1.4 (page 22). Think of the difference it will make when we create environments that develop deep learning, positive academic self-concepts, and student self-efficacy.

• • • • • ♥ • • • • •

I began this book by telling you a story.

I was the student sitting in Mr. Kelly's summer school classroom (page 1). I was not a reader or writer. To me, reading books was a burden. Picking up that book, *The Outsiders* (Hinton, 1967), started something. It was not a magical switch that turned me into a reader, but it was a first step in changing my academic self-concept.

I took the book home that evening. It was a Thursday, and the last day of the week for summer school. My parents had arranged a vacation with a group of close friends in what we called *up north* Michigan. We were leaving shortly after I was scheduled to get back from summer school. The bags were packed and in the van.

I remember jumping into the car, ready to go, and my mother asking me if I had my book. I did not. She told me to go back into the house and get it. I was unenthusiastic, but grabbed my copy. As we got onto the freeway to begin the four-hour drive, I opened the book and started reading it for real. I remember this because it was the first time I actually connected with a book. I read it cover to cover. I lost track of time. When the van stopped in Ludington, Michigan, I did not get out. I had to finish. *The Outsiders* was the first book I loved.

So began the development of my positive academic self-concept, which initiated the self-efficacy cycle, which made it possible for me to earn my PhD and write multiple books. Hinton's 1967 book was the catalyst for a journey that changed my life. It allowed me to learn something new about myself. Throughout high school, I experienced other cycles that contributed to my positive academic self-concept as a reader, but reading *that* book was the pivotal starting point. What experiences changed your academic self-concept and helped make you the educator you are?

You can manage engagement with the strategies presented in this book. What other methods can you try? You are an engaged, self-efficacious person who is interested in learning deeply. You will no doubt create and discover wonderful ideas during your quest to help your students love what they learn. To help make that change, use the self-reflective rubrics at the end of chapters 2–5. For assistance on your classroom culture growth, use the student engagement needs inventories and the "Teacher Self-Reflection—Artifacts" reproducible (page 134).

APPENDIX

ENGAGEMENT INVENTORIES

How would you characterize your students' cognitive and affective experience in your class? If you are a secondary teacher, do you see differences in engagement in different class periods? If you are an elementary teacher, does your students' engagement change outside of your class? How can you identify what your struggling students need?

You have read about the strategies, but where do you start? By asking your students to complete the inventory, you get to see engagement through their eyes. What are your students' perceptions about how engaging your class is? What element (or elements) of engagement do they need as a group?

Acting on the data you collect from the following reproducible inventories aids school improvement, discussions, and self-reflection. The inventories blend and adapt existing scientifically proven tools to evaluate student self-concept, self-determination, and motivation, but they *are not* formal teacher evaluations as required by many organizations. They provide data that teams and teachers can use to make informed decisions. You can use the resulting data to plan an engagement strategy and then, months later, administer it again to find out how engagement is growing. In addition to gaining helpful data, educators benefit from this tool because of how quickly they obtain the results. I have worked with multiple schools that use this inventory.

The tool is based on the self-determination theory (Ryan & Deci, 2000a, 2000b) that forms the framework for the previous chapters, and I adapted the engagement needs inventories from multiple tools (García-Ros et al., 2017; Green et al., 2006; Martin, 2007; Schilling, 2009; Snipes & Tran, 2017; Wang et al., 2014). Adapting these types of student engagement and motivation tools is common (O'Toole & Due, 2015). This adaptation is based on the model of engagement and academic self-concept continuum in figure 1.4 (page 22). You can see the engagement and academic self-concept continuum merged in figure A.1 (page 138).

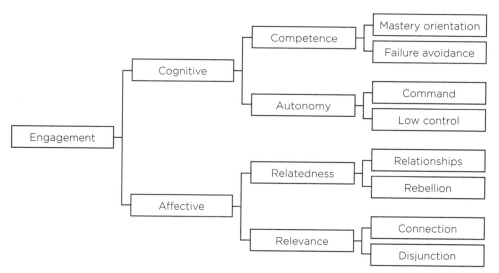

Source: Adapted from Martin, 2007; McInerney et al., 2012; Ryan & Deci, 2000a, 2000b; Shavelson et al., 1976.

FIGURE A.1: Engagement and academic self-concept continuum unified model.

The inventories have questions that provide information from all eight continuum elements: mastery orientation, failure avoidance, command, low control, relationships, rebellion, connection, and disjunction. The inventories are based on how students perceive their engagement experiences in your classroom and school. For each element, students in grades 4–12 rate their perceptions on a five-point scale: 5–Almost Always, 4–Most of the Time, 3–Sometimes, 2–Not Very Much, and 1–Almost Never (Schilling, 2009). Students in grades K–3 rate their perceptions with happy, sad, or neutral faces.

In many of the research studies from which these inventories are adapted, the questions were tested against self-efficacy levels or elements associated with positive academic self-concept. See the following points.

- All the questions on the positive, self-determination side had a statistically significant positive connection to the positive academic self-concepts developed in this book. This is important because these questions are scientifically proven to find out what students think about engagement.

- All the questions from the self-sabotage side have a statistically significant and negative connection with the positive academic self-concepts developed in this book. These questions are based on the academic self-concept and self-sabotage continuum in figure 1.3 (page 20) and reveal if a student self-sabotages. These questions help identify classes or students who immediately need intervention help for engagement.

- The only exceptions to the preceding descriptions in the following reproducibles are questions 7, 17, and 18, which I wrote and are currently untested in the research. They ask about specific classroom engagement artifacts or norms that have been scientifically proven to increase those specific elements of engagement.

Administering the Inventories

Do not give the inventories in the beginning of the school year. At that point, students are still adopting the classroom culture. The ideal time to give these inventories is anytime after six weeks of school, so students have a chance to adopt the classroom culture you developed. If you test before the students have been socialized to the norms, the inventory will not give you accurate results.

After at least six weeks, administer the inventory. Then choose and employ strategies from this book based on the results. Administer the inventories again, near the end of the semester or school year, to see possible changes in students' perceptions.

The inventories can be anonymous (without a student giving his or her name), which has the advantage of making sure input is completely honest. Or, you can ask students to include their names on the inventories, which has the benefit of customizing your responses to students who lack cognitive or affective engagement. It also helps you further compare data.

If students' names *are* on the inventories, you can pair school-level achievement data (from state assessments, iReady, STAR, or NWEA, for example) with engagement needs inventories. That enables large-scale instructional strategies, interventions, and professional development.

Choosing Approaches Based on Inventory Data

Using a tool to evaluate students' cognitive and affective elements is very important because teachers generally only judge a student's engagement through behavior (O'Toole & Due, 2015). This assessment provides quantifiable data. As mentioned in chapter 1 (page 7), teachers know engagement when they see it, but using the inventory helps distinguish needs.

You can find a specific element's score based on the metric that you, your collaborative team, your department or grade level, or even your entire school needs. It will allow you to see where your engagement cultures are and decide on the most import-ant aspects to work on together, be it cognitive or affective, competence, autonomy, relatedness, or relevance. Look for substantial differences. As you collate and graph the data, consider these questions: How do my students' perceptions differ from my perception of engagement? In what engagement element are my students' perceptions different from my own perception? What element should I increase in my classroom? You can develop collaborative teams around the four elements of engagement; review the corresponding chapter; find and agree on additional strategies to try for those elements; and support each other via instructional rounds. You also can develop strategies and pursue professional development around that topic.

You can also compare the students' perceptions to the rubrics you completed at the end of chapters 2–5. Even though the rubrics are on a four-point scale, it is easy to see where your students' perceptions about engagement both align with and diverge from your own.

You can use the following metrics.

- An overall mean can measure engagement, and by using the inventory a second time, you can gauge changes. Use this score at the building, department, or grade level to see a big picture.

- A mean among all cognitive-based questions reveals a need for more cognition-based strategies and is useful at a building, department, or grade level to compare and plan for cooperative learning. These are good data to use when introducing these engagement concepts. Imagine giving this inventory and producing the data for each class or department as you teach your team about the engagement components in this book.

- The competence and autonomy questions from the cognitive engagement element reveal students' perceptions of their own classroom-level engagement.

- The affective engagement outcome can be used on a classroom level to identify your students' level of affective connection to your class. It also is broken down to two different levels of relatedness to the teacher and relevance to the content.

- A breakdown is possible by individual item and then by class, grade, subject, school, or district.

Figure A.2 lays out the breakdown. Find an administrator or teacher in the school who can help with the scoring. Also, you could bring in a consultant to help admin-ister, score, and share the data with staff.

Overall Engagement Outcome Mean for Questions 1–30 (8–10, 19, 20, 29, 30 reversed)			
Cognitive Engagement Mean for Questions 1–20 (8–10, 19, 20 reversed)		**Affective Engagement** Mean for Questions 21–30 (29, 30 reversed)	
Breakdown by Individual Item			
Competence Questions 1–7	**Autonomy** Questions 11–18	**Relatedness** Questions 21–24	**Relevance** Questions 25–28

FIGURE A.2: Scoring for the student engagement needs inventories with question numbers.

*Visit **go.SolutionTree.com/instruction** for a free reproducible version of this figure.*

Score the inventories to the hundredth decimal. To find the mean for the overall engagement outcome, add all the students' scores from all thirty questions and then divide by 30.

Pay special attention to the questions labeled *Reversed*. Flip the scores for those questions *before* calculating the total. For reversed K–3 scores, tally a frowning face (1) as a 5 before calculating the mean. For a neutral face (3), the score stays as is. For reversed grades 4–12 scores, tally a 1 instead as a 5, a 2 instead as a 4, and vice versa. A 3 stays as is.

Chapter 2 focuses on students gaining competence. Questions 1–7 in both inventories test a student's perception of his or her growth mindset, the development of persistence behaviors, and the perceived presence of competence supports in the classroom. Questions 8–10 score students' perception of their failure avoidance. Again, note they are reversed, which means their scores will be flipped before calculating them into the mean. They are flipped because those questions ask students about their perceptions from a self-sabotaging standpoint; lower scores mean higher engagement for these questions specifically.

Chapter 3 focuses on strategies to build students' autonomy. Questions 11–18 focus on the sense of command a student feels in the class. They test for his or her ability to manage studies and plan and monitor learning. Questions 19 and 20 are related to students' feelings of low control. These items will also be reversed before scoring.

Chapters 4 and 5 focus on strategies to increase the level of relatedness students feel toward the teacher and the content being taught. Questions 21–24 test the student's perception of his or her connection to the teacher. Questions 25–28 test the students' perceived connection to the content. Questions 29 and 30 test the students' feelings of rebellion. Again, reverse the responses when calculating those questions' scores.

Student Engagement Needs Inventory— Grades K–3

This is a long process. Administer the inventory as follows.

- Read the inventory aloud to students in K–2; grade 3 students tend to have better reading skills.

- Question only one student at a time to avoid students' repeating each other's answers.

- Take breaks after ten questions.

- If a student doesn't answer after being asked twice, leave the question blank. Do not count it as an answer.

- You can administer sections over multiple days to avoid tiring them.

- The classroom teacher needn't be the interviewer. A staff member, interventionist, or paraprofessional can administer the inventory.

- Students choose among sad (no, not much), neutral (sometimes), and happy (yes, a lot) face images for their responses. Numbers make scoring easier.

- Even though using the entire population produces more precise data, consider taking a randomly selected sample for your class or grades K–3. Thirty samples are statistically enough to give a picture of your school's engagement.

Completing this inventory is difficult for kindergarteners, but you can still learn interesting things from their responses and their follow-up statements.

1—No, not much; 3—Sometimes; 5—Yes, a lot	☹ 1	😐 3	😊 5
1. If I don't understand my work at first, I keep trying until I understand it.			
2. I feel good about myself when I really understand what I'm learning.			
3. I think up new questions in my mind as we work in class.			
4. If I make a mistake, I try to figure out the right answer.			
5. I work with my classmates, and we learn from one another.			
6. I join in class discussions.			
7. In this class, I know my learning goals.			
8. The main reason I work is to not disappoint my parent or parents.			
9. In this class, sometimes I don't raise my hand or participate in discussions because I am afraid to seem silly.			

page 1 of 2

	😞 1	😐 3	😊 5
10. I would rather do easy work that I can do well than do things that are hard, where I might learn more.			
11. When I work at home, I work in a quiet place.			
12. Before I begin working in class, I make a plan to help make sure I do it right.			
13. I finish my assignments.			
14. I check my book, materials, or classroom posters to help me know what I'm learning.			
15. I turn in assignments on time.			
16. I come to class with all of my materials.			
17. In this class, I can show what I learned in different ways.			
18. The teacher listens to us about what the class is going to learn.			
19. In this class, I'm often unsure how I can avoid doing poorly.			
20. When tests and assignments are coming up in this class, I worry a lot.			
21. My teacher believes in me.			
22. Most mornings, I feel like going to school when I get up.			
23. I can count on my teacher to help me understand what I am learning.			
24. My teacher encourages me to try hard.			
25. The things I am learning are important to me.			
26. I feel content when I'm working.			
27. The things I am learning in class are interesting to me.			
28. What we learn in this class reminds me of things outside of school.			
29. I am afraid to try hard because I might not do well.			
30. My teacher doesn't care about me.			

Source: Adapted from García-Ros, R., Pérez-González, F., Tomás, J. M., & Fernández, I. (2017). The schoolwork engagement inventory: Factorial structure, measurement invariance by gender and educational level, and convergent validity in secondary education (12–18 years). Journal of Psychoeducational Assessment, 36(6), 588–603; Green, J., Nelson, G., Martin, A. J., & Marsh, H. (2006). The causal ordering of self-concept and academic motivation and its effect on academic achievement. International Education Journal, 7(4), 534–546; Martin, A. J. (2007). Examining a multidimensional model of student motivation and engagement using a construct validation approach. British Journal of Educational Psychology, 77(2), 413–440; Ng, C., Bartlett, B., & Elliott, S. N. (2018). Empowering engagement: Creating learning opportunities for students from challenging backgrounds. New York: Springer; Orkin, M., Pott, M., Wolf, M., May, S., & Brand, E. (2018). Beyond gold stars: Improving the skills and engagement of struggling readers through intrinsic motivation. Reading & Writing Quarterly, 34(3), 203–217; Parsons, S. A., Nuland, L. R., & Parsons, A. W. (2014). The ABCs of student engagement. Phi Delta Kappan, 95(8), 23–27; Schilling, J. C. (2009). A quantitative and qualitative investigation of variability and contextual sources related to the academic engagement of minority and economically disadvantaged adolescents. Published doctoral dissertation, University of Virginia, Charlottesville; Snipes, J., & Tran, L. (2017). Growth mindset, performance avoidance, and academic behaviors in Clark County School District (REL 2017–226). Washington, DC: Institute of Education Sciences; Wang, Z., Bergin, C., & Bergin, D. A. (2014). Measuring engagement in fourth to twelfth grade classrooms: The classroom engagement inventory. School Psychology Quarterly, 29(4), 517–535.

Student Engagement Needs Inventory—
Grades 4–12

In this class allows multiple teachers in a secondary school to give this inventory (Wang et al., 2014). Let students know that their answers should be honest and that none of the students' answers will be used against them, especially if the inventory will have their name on it. I highly suggest asking students their gender or other demographic differences you may have in your school so you can parse the data and target the strategies even further.

1—Never, 2—Almost Never, 3—Sometimes, 4—Almost Always, 5—Always	1	2	3	4	5
1. If I don't understand my work, I keep going over it until I understand it.					
2. In this class, I feel very pleased with myself when I really understand what I'm taught.					
3. I form new questions in my mind as I join in class activities.					
4. If I make a mistake, I try to figure out where I went wrong.					
5. In this class, I work with other students, and we learn from each other.					
6. In this class, I actively participate in class discussions.					
7. In this class, I know what our learning goal or target is.					
8. In this class, the main reason I work is to not disappoint my parents.					
9. In this class, sometimes I don't raise my hand or participate in discussions because I am afraid to seem foolish.					
10. I would rather do easy work that I can do well than challenging work where I might learn more.					
11. When I study for this class, I'm usually in places where I can concentrate.					
12. In this class, before I start an assignment, I plan out how I am going to do it.					
13. For this class, I complete my assignments.					
14. When I'm not sure about things, I check my book, materials, or items my teacher has displayed to help me.					
15. I turn in assignments on the due date.					

page 1 of 2

	1	2	3	4	5
16. I come to class with all of my materials.					
17. In this class, I can show what I learned in many different ways.					
18. The teacher listens to us about what the class is going to learn.					
19. In this class, I'm often unsure how I can avoid doing poorly.					
20. When exams and assignments are coming up in this class, I worry a lot.					
21. My teacher shows me that he or she believes I can do well in school.					
22. Most mornings, I feel like going to school when I get up.					
23. I can count on my teacher to help me understand what I am learning.					
24. In this class, my teacher encourages me to work hard.					
25. In this class, the work is important to me.					
26. In this class, I feel happy when I'm working.					
27. The work in my class is personally interesting to me.					
28. What we learn in this class reminds me of things outside of school.					
29. In this class, I don't study hard so I have an excuse if I don't do well on the tests.					
30. My teacher doesn't care if I think something is unfair.					

Source: Adapted from García-Ros, R., Pérez-González, F., Tomás, J. M., & Fernández, I. (2017). The schoolwork engagement inventory: Factorial structure, measurement invariance by gender and educational level, and convergent validity in secondary education (12–18 years). Journal of Psychoeducational Assessment, 36(6), 588–603; Green, J., Nelson, G., Martin, A. J., & Marsh, H. (2006). The causal ordering of self-concept and academic motivation and its effect on academic achievement. International Education Journal, 7(4), 534–546; Martin, A. J. (2007). Examining a multidimensional model of student motivation and engagement using a construct validation approach. British Journal of Educational Psychology, 77(2), 413–440; Ng, C., Bartlett, B., & Elliott, S. N. (2018). Empowering engagement: Creating learning opportunities for students from challenging backgrounds. *New York: Springer; Orkin, M., Pott, M., Wolf, M., May, S., & Brand, E. (2018). Beyond gold stars: Improving the skills and engagement of struggling readers through intrinsic motivation.* Reading & Writing Quarterly, 34(3), 203–217; Parsons, S. A., Nuland, L. R., & Parsons, A. W. (2014). The ABCs of student engagement. Phi Delta Kappan, 95(8), 23–27; Schilling, J. C. (2009). A quantitative and qualitative investigation of variability and contextual sources related to the academic engagement of minority and economically disadvantaged adolescents. *Published doctoral dissertation, University of Virginia, Charlottesville; Snipes, J., & Tran, L. (2017). Growth mindset, performance avoidance, and academic behaviors in Clark County School District (REL 2017–226). Washington, DC: Institute of Education Sciences; Wang, Z., Bergin, C., & Bergin, D. A. (2014). Measuring engagement in fourth to twelfth grade classrooms: The classroom engagement inventory.* School Psychology Quarterly, 29(4), 517–535.

Engagement Inventory Rubric

Using the inventories (pages 142–145) allows you to see how your students perceive your classroom. Their perceptions are their realities. If the scores conflict with your perceptions, look at your practice, starting with the strategies and concepts in this book.

Consider sharing these data with your students and getting their feedback on the data. Conversations with your students about the positive engagement elements from the inventories will only strengthen a student's level of relatedness. It is, of course, important that these conversations include listening to student feedback.

Calculate a classroom mean from students' inventory results and then calculate a mean from each of the teacher engagement rubrics at the end of chapters 2–5. On the left side is a five-point scale for the students' inventory and on the right is a four-point scale for the teacher rubric. Color in left and right columns to the students' level (left) and the teachers' level (right) to see a comparison.

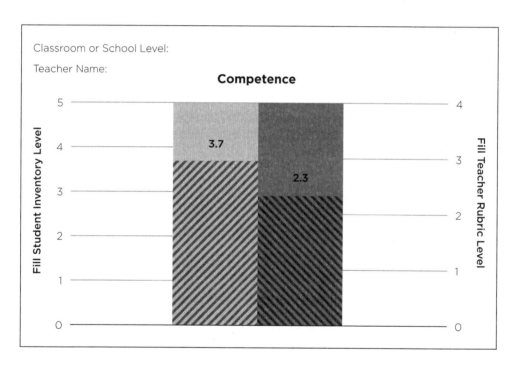

Classroom or School Level:

Teacher Name:

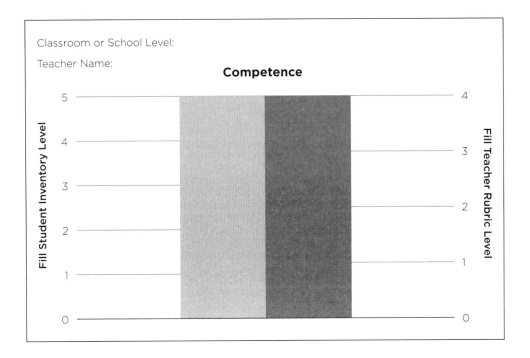

Classroom or School Level:

Teacher Name:

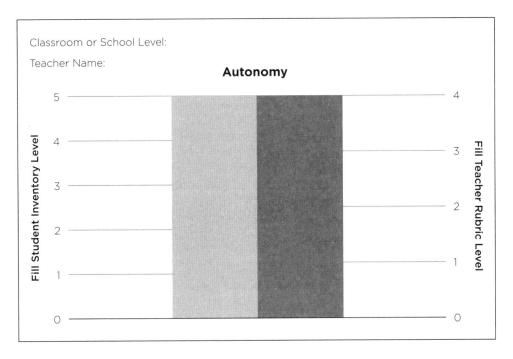

Classroom or School Level:

Teacher Name:

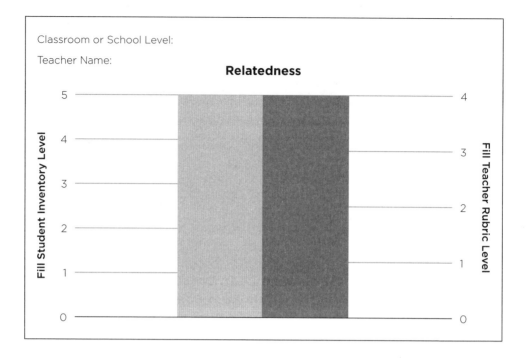

Classroom or School Level:

Teacher Name:

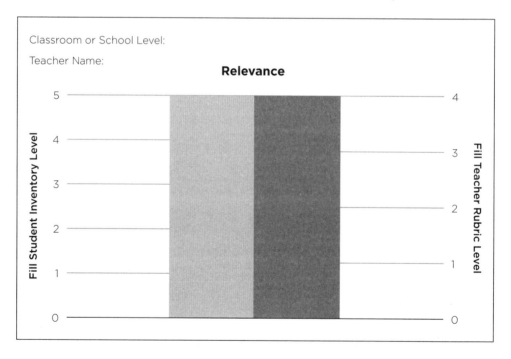

page 3 of 4

When the data are completely filled in, what do they tell you about each element of engagement?

Competence:

Autonomy:

Relatedness:

Relevance:

   You could bring together all the data from the school and use the same graph to see a whole-school view. If teachers feel they do have the classroom engagement culture artifacts in the rubric from a specific element, but the students' perceptions don't bear that out, this creates an excellent opportunity to collaborate about why the differences exist and how collaborative teams can support teachers to change the students' experiences. Also, when both have a lower score, teachers can go back to the chapter and discuss how to support one another with the strategies. If your staff and colleagues together decide on and implement strategies that support one another, engagement and learning increase (Orkin et al., 2018). Work together to transform your students' engagement and help them learn at higher levels.

Source: Orkin, M., Pott, M., Wolf, M., May, S., & Brand, E. (2018). Beyond gold stars: Improving the skills and engagement of struggling readers through intrinsic motivation. Reading & Writing Quarterly, *34(3), 203–217.*

REFERENCES AND RESOURCES

20-Time in Education. (n.d.). *Home*. Accessed at www.20timeineducation.com/home on August 30, 2019.

Abbott, A. L. (2017). Fostering student interest development: An engagement intervention. *Middle School Journal, 48*(3), 34–45.

Adler, I., Schwartz, L., Madjar, N., & Zion, M. (2018). Reading between the lines: The effect of contextual factors on student motivation throughout an open inquiry process. *Science Education, 102*(4), 820–855.

Ahmed, W., & Bruinsma, M. (2006). A structural model of self-concept, autonomous motivation and academic performance in cross-cultural perspective. *Electronic Journal of Research in Educational Psychology, 4*(3), 551–576.

Alderson-Day, B., & Fernyhough, C. (2015). Inner speech: Development, cognitive functions, phenomenology, and neurobiology. *Psychological Bulletin, 141*(5), 931–965. Accessed at www.ncbi.nlm.nih.gov/pmc/articles/PMC4538954 on June 10, 2019.

Al-Hendawi, M. (2012). Academic engagement of students with emotional and behavioral disorders: Existing research, issues, and future directions. *Emotional & Behavioural Difficulties, 17*(2), 125–141.

Andrade, H., & Du, Y. (2007). Student responses to criteria-referenced self-assessment. *Assessment & Evaluation in Higher Education, 32*(2), 159–181.

Anseel, F., Lievens, F., & Schollaert, E. (2009). Reflection as a strategy for enhancing the effect of feedback on task performance. *Organizational Behavior and Human Decision Processes, 110*, 23–35.

Appleton, J. J., Christenson, S. L., & Furlong, M. J. (2008). Student engagement with school: Critical conceptual and methodological issues of the construct. *Psychology in the Schools, 45*(5), 369–386.

Argyle, M. (1999). The development of social coping skills. In E. Frydenberg (Ed.), *Learning to cope: Developing as a person in complex societies* (pp. 81–106). Oxford, England: Oxford University Press.

Assor, A., Kaplan, H., Kanat-Maymon, Y., & Roth, G. (2005). Directly controlling teacher behaviors as predictors of poor motivation and engagement in girls and boys: The role of anger and anxiety. *Learning and Instruction*, *15*(5), 397–413.

Atencio, D. J. (2004). Structured autonomy or guided participation? Constructing interest and understanding in a lab activity. *Early Childhood Education Journal*, *31*(4), 233–239.

Bailey, A. L., & Heritage, M. (2018). *Self-regulation in learning: The role of language and formative assessment*. Cambridge, MA: Harvard Education Press.

Bailey, K., & Jakicic, C. (2012). *Common formative assessments: A toolkit for Professional Learning Communities at Work*. Bloomington, IN: Solution Tress Press.

Barber, A. T., & Buehl, M. M. (2012). Relations among grade 4 students' perceptions of autonomy, engagement in science, and reading motivation. *Journal of Experimental Education*, *81*(1), 22–43.

Barkaoui, K., Barrett, S. E., Samaroo, J., Dahya, N., Alidina, S., & James, C. E. (2015). Teachers' conceptions of student engagement in learning: The case of three urban schools. *Alberta Journal of Educational Research*, *61*(1), 80–99.

Basten, M., Meyer-Ahrens, I., Fries, S., & Wilde, M. (2014). The effects of autonomy-supportive vs. controlling guidance on learners' motivational and cognitive achievement in a structured field trip. *Science Education*, *98*(6), 1033–1053.

Baumeister, R. F., & Leary, M. R. (1995). The need to belong: Desire for interpersonal attachments as a fundamental human motivation. *Psychological Bulletin*, *117*(3), 497–529.

Beesley, A. D., Clark, T. F., Dempsey, K., & Tweed, A. (2018). Enhancing formative assessment practice and encouraging middle school mathematics engagement and persistence. *School Science and Mathematics*, *118*(1–2), 4–16.

Benson, C. (n.d.). *School-wide events*. Accessed at https://mascmahs.org/school-wide-events on June 12, 2019.

Bigelman, L. G., & Peterson, D. S. (2016). *No more reading instruction without differentiation*. Portsmouth, NH: Heinemann.

Black, P., & Wiliam, D. (1998a). Assessment and classroom learning: Principles, policy & practice. *Assessment in Education*, *5*(1), 7–74.

Black, P., & Wiliam, D. (1998b). Inside the black box: Raising standards through classroom assessment. *Phi Delta Kappan*, *80*(2), 139–148.

Blackwell, L. S., Trzesniewski, K. H., & Dweck, C. S. (2007). Implicit theories of intelligence predict achievement across an adolescent transition: A longitudinal study and an intervention. *Child Development*, *78*(1), 246–263.

Bolton, F. C. (2006). Rubrics and adult learners: Andragogy and assessment. *Assessment Update*, *18*(3), 5–6.

Brint, S., & Cantwell, A. M. (2014). Conceptualizing, measuring, and analyzing the characteristics of academically disengaged students: Results from UCUES 2010. *Journal of College Student Development, 55*(8), 808–823.

Bronfenbrenner, U. (1974). The origins of alienation. *Scientific American, 231*(2), 53–61.

Brookhart, S. M. (2013). *How to create and use rubrics for formative assessment and grading.* Alexandria, VA: Association for Supervision and Curriculum Development.

Brown, J. R. (2014). Hook and hold. *Teaching Children Mathematics, 21*(1), 47–54.

Buckner, E., Shores, M., Sloane, M., Dantzler, J., Shields, C., Shader, K. et al. (2016). Honors and non-honors student engagement: A model of student, curricular, and institutional characteristics. *Journal of the National Collegiate Honors Council, 17*(1), 191–217.

Burgess, D. (2012). *Teach like a pirate: Increase student engagement, boost your creativity, and transform your life as an educator.* San Diego, CA: Burgess Consulting.

Cairns, R. B., & Cairns, B. D. (1994). *Lifelines and risks: Pathways of youth in our time.* Cambridge, England: Cambridge University Press.

Canning, E. A., Harackiewicz, J. M., Priniski, S. J., Hecht, C. A., Tibbetts, Y., & Hyde, J. S. (2018). Improving performance and retention in introductory biology with a utility-value intervention. *Journal of Educational Psychology, 110*(6), 834–849.

Cardwell, M. E. (2011). *Patterns of relationships between teacher engagement and student engagement.* Published doctoral dissertation, St. John Fisher College, Rochester, NY.

Carnegie, D. (1937). *How to win friends and influence people.* New York: Simon & Schuster.

Carnes, M., Devine, P. G., Isaac, C., Manwell, L. B., Ford, C. E., Byars-Winston, A., et al. (2012). Promoting institutional change through bias literacy. *Journal of Diverse High Education, 5*(2), 63–77. Accessed at www.ncbi.nlm.nih.gov/pmc/articles/PMC3399596 on June 12, 2019.

Cayanus, J. L., & Martin, M. M. (2008). Teacher self-disclosure: Amount, relevance and negativity. *Communication Quarterly, 56*, 325–341.

Cayanus, J. L., Martin, M. M., & Goodboy, A. K. (2009). The relation between teacher self-disclosure and student motives to communicate. *Communication Research Reports, 26*(2), 105–113.

Center for Mental Health in Schools at UCLA. (2004). *Addressing barriers to learning.* Los Angeles: Author.

Center on the Developing Child. (n.d.). *Executive function & self-regulation.* Accessed at https://developingchild.harvard.edu/science/key-concepts/executive-function on April 22, 2019.

Chapman, C., & Vagle, N. (2011). *Motivating students: 25 strategies to light the fire of engagement.* Bloomington, IN: Solution Tree Press.

Cheng, E. (n.d.). *Teacher bias and its impact on teacher-student relationships: The example of favoritism.* Accessed at http://smhp.psych.ucla.edu/pdfdocs/teacherbias.pdf on August 30, 2019.

City, E. A., Elmore, R. F., Fiarman, S. E., & Teitel, L. (2009). *Instructional rounds in education: A network approach to improving teaching and learning.* Cambridge, MA: Harvard Education Press.

Coffey, S., Anyinam, C., & Zitzelsberger, H. (2018). Meaningful engagement with academic integrity through a focus on context and relationship. *New Directions for Community Colleges, 2018*(183), 15–23.

Coleman, C., & Davies, K. (2018). Striking gold: Introducing drama-maths. *Teachers and Curriculum, 18*(1), 9–18.

College Board. (n.d.). *Voting rates by age and education level, 2008.* Accessed at https://trends.collegeboard.org/education-pays/figures-tables/voting-rates-age-and-education-level-2008 on May 30, 2019.

Connell, J. P., & Wellborn, J. G. (1991). Competence, autonomy, and relatedness: A motivational analysis of self-system processes. In M. R. Gunnar & L. A. Sroufe (Eds.), *Self processes and development: The Minnesota symposia on child psychology, vol. 23* (pp. 43–77). Hillsdale, NJ: Erlbaum.

Corso, M. J., Bundick, M. J., Quaglia, R. J., & Haywood, D. E. (2013). Where student, teacher, and content meet: Student engagement in the secondary school classroom. *American Secondary Education, 41*(3), 50–61.

Cowen, E. L., & Work, W. C. (1988). Resilient children, psychological wellness, and primary prevention. *American Journal of Community Psychology, 16*(4), 591–607.

Cox, A., & Williams, L. (2008). The roles of perceived teacher support, motivational climate, and psychological need satisfaction in students' physical education motivation. *Journal of Sport and Exercise Psychology, 30*(2), 222–239.

Creative Educator. (n.d.). *Classroom constitution.* Accessed at https://creativeeducator.tech4learning.com/2016/lessons/classroom-constitution on April 19, 2019.

Crumpton, H. E., & Gregory, A. (2011). "I'm not learning": The role of academic relevancy for low-achieving students. *Journal of Educational Research, 104*(1), 42–53.

Csikszentmihalyi, M. (1975). *Beyond boredom and anxiety.* San Francisco: Jossey-Bass.

Csikszentmihalyi, M. (1991). Literacy and intrinsic motivation. In *How we think and learn: A lecture series* (pp. 35–40). Washington, DC: National Council on Vocational Education.

Csikszentmihalyi, M. (2008). *Flow: The psychology of optimal experience.* New York: Harper Perennial.

Daniel, J. R., & Cooc, N. (2018). Teachers' perceptions of academic intrinsic motivation for students with disabilities. *Journal of Special Education, 52*(2), 101–112.

Davidson, A. J., Gest, S. D., & Welsh, J. A. (2010). Relatedness with teachers and peers during early adolescence: An integrated variable-oriented and person-oriented approach. *Journal of School Psychology*, *48*(6), 483–510.

Davis, E. A. (2003). Prompting middle school science students for productive reflection: Generic and directed prompts. *Journal of the Learning Sciences*, *12*(1), 91–142.

de Boer, H., Bosker, R. J., & Van der Werf, M. P. C. (2010). Sustainability of teacher expectation bias effects on long-term student performance. *Journal of Educational Psychology*, *102*(1), 168–179.

Dean, C. B., Hubbell, E. R., Pitler, H., & Stone, B. (2012). *Classroom instruction that works: Research-based strategies for increasing student achievement* (2nd ed.). Alexandria, VA: Association for Supervision and Curriculum Development.

Dean, D., & Kuhn, D. (2007). Direct instruction vs. discovery: The long view. *Science Education*, *91*, 384–397.

Deci, E. L., & Ryan, R. M. (2014). Autonomy and need satisfaction in close relationships: Relationships motivation theory. In N. Weinstein (Ed.), *Human motivation and interpersonal relationships: Theory, research, and applications* (pp. 53–73). Dordrecht, the Netherlands: Springer.

Dee, T. S. (2004). The race connection. *Education Next*, *4*(2), 53–59.

Deed, D. (2008). Disengaged boys' perspectives about learning. *Journal of Education*, *36*(1), 3–14.

Denson, N. (2009). Do curricular and co-curricular diversity activities influence racial bias? A meta-analysis. *Review of Educational Research*, *79*(2), 805–838.

DePasquale, J. (2017, July 21). *Student interest surveys: Getting to know you* [Blog post]. Accessed at www.scholastic.com/teachers/blog-posts/john-depasquale/2017/Student -Interest-Surveys-Getting-to-Know-You on April 16, 2019.

Desautel, D. (2009). Becoming a thinking thinker: Metacognition, self-reflection, and classroom practice. *Teachers College Record*, *111*(8), 1997–2020.

Dewey, J. (1933). *How we think: A restatement of the relation of reflective thinking to the educative process*. Boston: D.C. Heath.

Di Stefano, G., Gino, F., Pisano, G. P., & Staats, B. R. (2016). *Making experience count: The role of reflection in individual learning* (Harvard Business School NOM Unit Working Paper No. 14–093). Accessed at https://papers.ssrn.com/sol3/papers.cfm?abstract_id=2414478 on April 16, 2019.

Diab, R., & Balaa, L. (2011). Developing detailed rubrics for assessing critique writing: Impact on EFL university students' performance and attitudes. *TESOL Journal*, *2*(1), 52–72.

DuFour, R., DuFour, R., Eaker, R., Many, T. W., & Mattos, M. (2016). *Learning by doing: A handbook for Professional Learning Communities at Work* (3rd ed.). Bloomington, IN: Solution Tree Press.

DuFour, R., DuFour, R., Lopez, D., & Muhammad, A. (2006). Promises kept: Collective commitments to students become a catalyst for improved professional practice. *Journal of Staff Development, 27*(3), 53–56.

Duijnhouwer, H., Prins, F. J., & Stokking, K. M. (2012). Feedback providing improvement strategies and reflection on feedback use: Effects on students' writing motivation, process, and performance. *Learning and Instruction, 22*(3), 171–184.

Duquette, G. (1995). *Second language practice: Classroom strategies for developing communicative competence.* Clevedon, England: Multilingual Matters.

Dweck, C. S. (2006). *Mindset: The new psychology of success.* New York: Ballantine Books.

Dweck, C. S. (2015). *Carol Dweck revisits the 'growth mindset'.* Accessed at www.edweek.org/ew/articles/2015/09/23/carol-dweck-revisits-the-growth-mindset.html on July 29, 2019.

Dweck, C. S., & Leggett, E. L. (1988). A social-cognitive approach to motivation and personality. *Psychological Review, 95*(2), 256–273.

Encyclopedia Britannica. (n.d.). *How a rejected block of marble became the world's most famous statue.* Accessed at www.britannica.com/story/how-a-rejected-block-of-marble-became-the-worlds-most-famous-statue on April 19, 2019.

Ely, R., Ainley, M., & Pearce, J. (2013). More than enjoyment: Identifying the positive affect component of interest that supports student engagement and achievement. *Middle Grades Research Journal, 8*(1), 13–32.

Estell, D. B., Farmer, T. W., & Cairns, B. D. (2007). Bullies and victims in rural African American youth: Behavioral characteristics and social network placement. *Aggressive Behavior, 33*(2), 145–159.

Farmer, T. W., Hall, C. M., Weiss, M. P., Petrin, R. A., Meece, J. L., & Moohr, M. (2011). The school adjustment of rural adolescents with and without disabilities: Variable and person-centered approaches. *Journal of Child and Family Studies, 20*(1), 78–88.

Farr, S. (2010). *Teaching as leadership: The highly effective teacher's guide to closing the achievement gap.* San Francisco: Jossey-Bass.

Farrington, C. A., Roderick, M., Allensworth, E., Nagaoka, J., Keyes, T. S., Johnson, D. W. et al. (2012). *Teaching adolescents to become learners: The role of noncognitive factors in shaping school performance—A critical literature review.* Chicago: University of Chicago Consortium on Chicago School Research.

Fedesco, H. N., Kentner, A., & Natt, J. (2017). The effect of relevance strategies on student perceptions of introductory courses. *Communication Education, 66*(2), 196–209.

Ferguson, R. F. (2011). *Tripod classroom-level student perceptions as measures of teaching effectiveness.* Accessed at www.dpi.state.nc.us/docs/effectiveness-model/surveys/ferguson -present.pdf on April 17, 2019.

Ferguson, R. F., Phillips, S. F., Rowley, J. F. S., & Friedlander, J. W. (2015). *The influence of teaching: Beyond standardized test scores—Engagement, mindsets, and agency.* Accessed at www.agi.harvard.edu/projects/TeachingandAgency.pdf on April 17, 2019.

Ferla, J., Valcke, M., & Cai, Y. (2009). Academic self-efficacy and academic self-concept: Reconsidering structural relationships. *Learning and Individual Differences, 19*(4), 499–505.

Ferlazzo, L. (2009). *Answers to "What do you do on the first day of school?"* Accessed at http:// larryferlazzo.edublogs.org/2009/08/09/answers-to-what-do-you-do-on-the-first-day-of -school on April 16, 2019.

Fisher, A. V., Godwin, K. E., & Seltman, H. (2014). Visual environment, attention allocation, and learning in young children: When too much of a good thing may be bad. *Psychological Science, 25*(7), 1362–1370.

Fisher, D., & Frey, N. (2008). *Better learning through structured teaching: A framework for the gradual release of responsibility.* Alexandria, VA: Association for Supervision and Curriculum Development.

Fisher, D., & Frey, N. (2015). *Unstoppable Learning: Seven essential elements to unleash student potential.* Bloomington, IN: Solution Tree Press.

Fisher, D., Frey, N., & Hattie, J. (2016). *Visible learning for literacy, grades K–12: Implementing the practices that work best to accelerate student learning.* Thousand Oaks, CA: SAGE.

Fisher, D., Frey, N., & Lapp, D. (2011). Focusing on the participation and engagement gap: A case study on closing the achievement gap. *Journal of Education for Students Placed at Risk, 16*(1), 56–64.

Flynn, N. (2007). What do effective teachers of literacy do? Subject knowledge and pedagogical choices for literacy. *Literacy, 41*(3), 137–146.

Fonseca, J., Carvalho, C., Conboy, J., Valente, M. O., Gama, A. P., Salema, M. H. et al. (2015). Changing teachers' feedback practices: A workshop challenge. *Australian Journal of Teacher Education, 40*(8), 59–82.

Fontanez, K. (2017). *Examining the impact of art-based anchor charts on academic achievement in language arts.* Published doctoral dissertation, Walden University, Minneapolis, MN.

Ford, J. K., Smith, E. M., Weissbein, D. A., Gully, S. M., & Salas, E. (1998). Relationships of goal orientation, metacognitive activity, and practice strategies with learning outcomes and transfer. *Journal of Applied Psychology, 83*(2), 218–233.

Fredricks, J. A., Blumenfeld, P. C., & Paris, A. H. (2004). School engagement: Potential of the concept, state of the evidence. *Review of Educational Research, 74*(1), 59–109.

Freeman, S., Eddy, S. L., McDonough, M., Smith, M. K., Okoroafor, N., Jordt, H., et al. (2014). Active learning increases student performance in science, engineering, and mathematics. *Proceedings of the National Academy of Sciences of the United States of America, 111*(23), 8410–8415.

Frymier, A. B., & Shulman, G. M. (1995). 'What's in it for me?': Increasing content relevance to enhance students' motivation. *Communication Education, 44*(1), 40–50.

Furrer, C., & Skinner, E. (2003). Sense of relatedness as a factor in children's academic engagement and performance. *Journal of Educational Psychology, 95*(1), 148–162.

Furrer, C. J., Skinner, E. A., & Pitzer, J. R. (2014). The influence of teacher and peer relationships on students' classroom engagement and everyday motivational resilience. *Teachers College Record, 116*(13), 101–123.

Furtak, E. M., & Kunter, M. (2012). Effects of autonomy-supportive teaching on student learning and motivation. *Journal of Experimental Education, 80*(3), 284–316.

Fyfe, E. R., Rittle-Johnson, B., & DeCaro, M. S. (2012). The effects of feedback during exploratory mathematics problem solving: Prior knowledge matters. *Journal of Educational Psychology, 104*(4), 1094–1108.

Gaede, S. D. (1985). *Belonging: Our need for community in church and family*. Grand Rapids, MI: Zondervan.

García-Ros, R., Pérez-González, F., Tomás, J. M., & Fernández, I. (2017). The schoolwork engagement inventory: Factorial structure, measurement invariance by gender and educational level, and convergent validity in secondary education (12–18 years). *Journal of Psychoeducational Assessment, 36*(6), 588–603.

Gilliam, W. S., Maupin, A. N., Reyes, C. R., Accavitti, M., & Shic, F. (2016). *Do early educators' implicit biases regarding sex and race relate to behavior expectations and recommendations of preschool expulsions and suspensions?* Accessed at https://pdfs.semanticscholar .org/95eb/66c67cd968551df29f7e374c1a253bd6b8ce.pdf?_ga=2.85233241.1962729428 .1570572798-62634307.1566913540 on October 8, 2019.

Gillies, R. M., & Boyle, M. (2005). Teachers' scaffolding behaviours during cooperative learning. *Asia-Pacific Journal of Teacher Education, 33*(3), 243–259.

Gillies, R. M., & Khan, A. (2008). The effects of teacher discourse on students' discourse, problem-solving and reasoning during cooperative learning. *International Journal of Educational Research, 47*(6), 323–340.

Gladwell, M. (2005). *Blink: The power of thinking without thinking*. New York: Little, Brown and Company.

Glover, S., Burns, J., Butler, H., & Patten, G. (1998). Social environments and the emotional wellbeing of young people. *Family Matters, 49*, 11–16.

Good, C., Aronson, J., & Inzlicht, M. (2003). Improving adolescents' standardized test performance: An intervention to reduce the effects of stereotype threat. *Journal of Applied Developmental Psychology, 24*(6), 645–662.

Goodenow, C. (1993). Classroom belonging among early adolescent students: Relationships to motivation and achievement. *Journal of Early Adolescence, 13*(1), 21–43.

Green, J., Nelson, G., Martin, A. J., & Marsh, H. (2006). The causal ordering of self-concept and academic motivation and its effect on academic achievement. *International Education Journal, 7*(4), 534–546.

Grolnick, W. S., Ryan, R. M., & Deci, E. L. (1991). Inner resources for school achievement: Motivational mediators of children's perceptions of their parents. *Journal of Educational Psychology, 83*(4), 508–517.

Guan, J. (2017). *Education in Australia*. Accessed at https://wenr.wes.org/2017/12/education-in-australia on April 17, 2019.

Guay, F., Larose, S., & Boivin, M. (2004). Academic self-concept and educational attainment level: A ten-year longitudinal study. *Self and Identity, 3*(1), 53–68.

Gurin, P. Y., Dey, E. L., Hurtado, S., & Gurin, G. (2002). Diversity and higher education: Theory and impact on educational outcomes. *Harvard Educational Review, 72*(3), 330–336.

Gutman, L. M., & Sulzby, E. (2000). The role of autonomy-support versus control in the emergent writing behaviors of African-American kindergarten children. *Reading Research and Instruction, 39*(2), 170–184.

Gwyn, L. P. (2004). *Sustained engagement in mathematics for elementary school learners: A narrative study of the relationship between classroom practices and incidence of flow learning situations for third- and fifth-grade gifted mathematics learners, or, traveling from Vegemite to gorilla*. Published doctoral dissertation, University of Missouri–St. Louis.

Hackathorn, J., Garczynski, A. M., Blankmeyer, K., Tennial, R. D., & Solomon, E. D. (2011). All kidding aside: Humor increases learning at knowledge and comprehension levels. *Journal of the Scholarship of Teaching and Learning, 11*(4), 116–123.

Haerens, L., Aelterman, N., Van den Berghe, L., De Meyer, J., Soenens, B., & Vansteenkiste, M. (2013). Observing physical education teachers' need-supportive interactions in classroom settings. *Journal of Sport and Exercise Psychology, 35*(1), 3–7.

Haimovitz, K., & Dweck, C. S. (2017). The origins of children's growth and fixed mindsets: New research and a new proposal. *Child Development, 88*(6), 1849–1859.

Hale, M. S., & City, E. A. (2006). *The teacher's guide to leading student-centered discussions: Talking about texts in the classroom*. Thousand Oaks, CA: SAGE.

Hampes, W. P. (2009). The relationship between humor and trust. *International Journal of Humor Research, 12*(3), 253–260.

Harbour, K. E., Evanovich, L. L., Sweigart, C. A., & Hughes, L. E. (2015). A brief review of effective teaching practices that maximize student engagement. *Preventing School Failure, 59*(1), 5–13.

Harper, E. (2007). Making good choices: How autonomy support influences the behavior change and motivation of troubled and troubling youth. *Reclaiming Children and Youth: The Journal of Strength-Based Interventions, 16*(3), 23–28.

Harris, M. J., & Rosenthal, R. (2005). No more teachers' dirty looks: Effects of teacher nonverbal behavior on student outcomes. In R. E. Riggio & R. S. Feldman (Eds.), *Applications of nonverbal communication* (pp. 157–192). Mahwah, NJ: Erlbaum.

Hart, R. A. (1992). *Children's participation: From tokenism to citizenship.* Florence, Italy: UNICEF International Child Development Centre. Accessed at www.unicef-irc.org /publications/pdf/childrens_participation.pdf on April 22, 2019.

Hart, S., Stewart, K., & Jimerson, S. (2011). The Student Engagement in Schools Questionnaire (SESQ) and the Teacher Engagement Report Form-New (TERF-N): Examining the preliminary evidence. *Contemporary School Psychology, 15*(1), 67–79.

Hastie, P., & Siedentop, D. (2006). The classroom ecology paradigm. In D. Kirk, D. MacDonald, & M. O'Sullivan (Eds.), *The handbook of physical education* (pp. 214–225). Thousand Oaks, CA: SAGE.

Hattie, J. (2002). Classroom composition and peer effects. *International Journal of Educational Research, 37*(5), 449–481.

Hattie, J. (2012). *Visible learning for teachers: Maximizing impact on learning.* London: Routledge.

Heick, T. (2017, August 23). *10 assessments you can perform in 90 seconds* [Blog post]. Accessed at www.teachthought.com/pedagogy/10-assessments-you-can-perform-in-90 -seconds on April 17, 2019.

Heick, T. (2018, March 18). *8 reflective questions to help any student think about their learning* [Blog post]. Accessed at www.teachthought.com/learning/use-twitter-exit-slip-teaching on April 17, 2019.

Hidi, S., & Renninger, K. A. (2006). The four-phase model of interest development. *Educational Psychologist, 41*(2), 111–127.

Hinton, S. E. (1967). *The outsiders.* New York: Viking.

Hirsch, S. E., Ennis, R. P., & Driver, M. K. (2018). Three student engagement strategies to help elementary teachers work smarter, not harder, in mathematics. *Beyond Behavior, 27*(1), 5–14.

Hosek, A. M. (n.d.). *Effective instructional practice: Using content relevance.* Accessed at www .natcom.org/sites/default/files/pages/EIP_Using_Content_Relevance.pdf on June 1, 2019.

Jackson, Y. (2011). *The pedagogy of confidence: Inspiring high intellectual performance in urban schools.* New York: Teachers College Press.

James, M., Black, P., Carmichael, P., Conner, C., Dudley, P., Fox, A. et al. (2006). *Learning how to learn: Tools for schools.* London: Routledge.

Jamison, R. S. (2014). *A longitudinal analysis of teacher vs. student reports of teacher-student relatedness and their relation to engagement across the transition to middle school.* Published doctoral dissertation, University of Illinois at Urbana-Champaign.

Jensen, E. (2019). *Poor students, rich teaching: Seven high-impact mindsets for students from poverty* (Rev. ed.). Bloomington, IN: Solution Tree Press.

Jones, S., Weissbourd, R., Bouffard, S., Kahn, J., & Anderson, T. R. (2018). *For educators: How to build empathy and strengthen your school community.* Accessed at https://mcc.gse .harvard.edu/resources-for-educators/how-build-empathy-strengthen-school-community on September 3, 2019.

Jonsson, A., & Svingby, G. (2007). The use of scoring rubrics: Reliability, validity and educational consequences. *Educational Research Review, 2*(2), 130–144.

Kanevsky, L. (2011). Deferential differentiation: What types of differentiation do students want? *Gifted Child Quarterly, 55*(4), 279–299.

Kaplan, H. (2018). Teachers' autonomy support, autonomy suppression and conditional negative regard as predictors of optimal learning experience among high-achieving Bedouin students. *Social Psychology of Education, 21*(1), 223–255.

Kaufman, P., Alt, M. N., & Chapman, C. D. (2001). *Dropout rates in the United States: 2000.* Accessed at http://nces.ed.gov/pubsearch/pubsinfo.asp?pubid=2002114 on April 19, 2019.

Keller, J. M. (1983). Motivational design of instruction. In C. M. Reigeluth (Ed.), *Instructional design theories: An overview of their current status* (pp. 383–434). Hillsdale, NJ: Erlbaum.

Kelley, L. (2018). Solution stories: A narrative study of how teachers support children's problem solving. *Early Childhood Education Journal, 46*(3), 313–322.

Kemb, P. B. (2017). *Fostering self-determination in students with intellectual disabilities: Secondary special education teachers' self-reported approaches, barriers, and support needs.* Published doctoral dissertation, Northcentral University, Prescott Valley, AZ.

Killian, S. (2017). *Hattie's 2017 updated list of factors influencing student achievement.* Accessed at https://theechochamberinternational.wordpress.com/2017/09/24/hatties -2017-updated-list-of-factors-influencing-student-achievement-shaun-killian on April 19, 2019.

Kinne, L. J., Hasenbank, J. F., & Coffey, D. (2014). Are we there yet? Using rubrics to support progress toward proficiency and model formative assessment. *AILACTE Journal, 11*(1), 109–128.

Kranzow, J., & Foote, S. M. (2018). Engaging sophomores through curricular and cocurricular initiatives. *New Directions for Higher Education, 2018*(183), 71–83.

Lam, S.-F., Jimerson, S., Kikas, E., Cefai, C., Veiga, F. H., Nelson, B. et al. (2012). Do girls and boys perceive themselves as equally engaged in school? The results of an international study from 12 countries. *Journal of School Psychology, 50*(1), 77–94.

Lazar, A. (2006). Literacy teachers making a difference in urban schools: A context-specific look at effective literacy teaching. *Journal of Reading Education*, *32*(1), 13–21.

Legault, L., Green-Demers, I., & Pelletier, L. (2006). Why do high school students lack motivation in the classroom? Toward an understanding of academic amotivation and the role of social support. *Journal of Educational Psychology*, *98*(3), 567–582.

Lehman, J. F., & Fisher, A. (2004). Dynamic curriculum delivery. *Community College Journal*, *74*(5), 60–62.

Lesley University. (n.d.). *The psychology of emotional and cognitive empathy*. Accessed at https://lesley.edu/article/the-psychology-of-emotional-and-cognitive-empathy on September 3, 2019.

Lietaert, S., Roorda, D., Laevers, F., Verschueren, K., & De Fraine, B. (2015). The gender gap in student engagement: The role of teachers' autonomy support, structure, and involvement. *British Journal of Educational Psychology*, *85*(4), 498–518.

Ling, L. T. Y. (2018). Meaningful gamification and students' motivation: A strategy for scaffolding reading material. *Online Learning Journal*, *22*(2), 141–155.

Livdahl, B. J. (1991). The learner-centered classroom: Explorations into language and learning. *Insights into Open Education*, *24*(1), 2–9.

Livingston, S. (2017). *Motivation and student success in developmental education*. Published doctoral dissertation, Edgewood College, Madison, WI.

Loera, G., Rueda, R., & Oh, Y. J. (2015). Learning and motivational characteristics of urban Latino high school youth. *Urban Education*, *53*(7), 875–898.

Lohbeck, A. (2016). Self-concept and self-determination theory: Math self-concept, motivation, and grades in elementary school children. *Early Child Development and Care*, *188*(8), 1031–1044.

Lord, C. (2016, May 6). *Ted Miltenberger: A legacy of ensemble* [Blog post]. Accessed at https://claudelord.org/2016/05/06/ted-miltenberger-a-legacy-of-ensemble-2 on April 23, 2019.

MacSuga-Gage, A. S., Simonsen, B., & Briere, D. E. (2012). Effective teaching practices that promote a positive classroom environment. *Beyond Behavior*, *22*(1), 14–22.

Mangiante, E. M. S. (2011). Teachers matter: Measures of teacher effectiveness in low-income minority schools. *Educational Assessment, Evaluation and Accountability*, *23*(1), 41–63.

Margolis, H., & McCabe, P. P. (2006). Improving self-efficacy and motivation: What to do, what to say. *Intervention in School and Clinic*, *41*(4), 218–227.

Marks, H. M. (2000). Student engagement in instructional activity: Patterns in the elementary, middle, and high school years. *American Educational Research Journal*, *37*(1), 153–184.

Marsh, H. W. (1991). Failure of high-ability schools to deliver academic benefits commensurate with their students' ability levels. *American Educational Research Journal*, *28*(2), 445–480.

Marsh, H. W., & Yeung, A. S. (1997). Coursework selection: Relations to academic self-concept and achievement. *American Educational Research Journal*, *34*(4), 691–720.

Marshik, T., Ashton, P. T., & Algina, J. (2017). Teachers' and students' needs for autonomy, competence, and relatedness as predictors of students' achievement. *Social Psychology of Education, 20*(1), 39–67.

Martin, A. J. (2003). The student motivation scale: Further testing of an instrument that measures school students' motivation. *Australian Journal of Education, 47*(1), 88–106.

Martin, A. J. (2007). Examining a multidimensional model of student motivation and engagement using a construct validation approach. *British Journal of Educational Psychology, 77*(2), 413–440.

Martin, A. J., & Dowson, M. (2009). Interpersonal relationships, motivation, engagement, and achievement: Yields for theory, current issues, and educational practice. *Review of Educational Research, 79*(1), 327–365.

Martin, E. R. (2012). Using self-determination theory to examine the difference in motivation of African American college students and students with other ethnic backgrounds. *Ursidae: The Undergraduate Research Journal at the University of Northern Colorado, 2*(2), 24–35.

Marzano, R. J. (2007). *The art and science of teaching: A comprehensive framework for effective instruction.* Alexandria, VA: Association for Supervision and Curriculum Development.

Marzano, R. J., & Pickering, D. J. (2011). *The highly engaged classroom.* Bloomington, IN: Marzano Resources.

Maurer, L. (n.d.). *School-wide events.* Accessed at https://mascmahs.org/school-wide-events on June 12, 2019.

McCarthy, J. R., & Edwards, R. (2011). *Key concepts in family studies.* Thousand Oaks, CA: SAGE.

McCarthy, M. E., Pretty, G. M., & Catano, V. (1990). Psychological sense of community and student burnout. *Journal of College Student Development, 31*(3), 211–216.

McInerney, D. M., Cheng, R. W., Mok, M. M. C., & Lam, A. K. H. (2012). Academic self-concept and learning strategies: Direction of effect on student academic achievement. *Journal of Advanced Academics, 23*(3), 249–269.

McLeod, S. (2018). *Lev Vygotsky.* Accessed at www.simplypsychology.org/vygotsky.html on April 19, 2019.

McNeece, A. (2009). *Sam Iver: Imminent threat.* Bloomington, IN: iUniverse.

McNeece, A. (2017). *Michigan's quantitative school culture inventories and student achievement.* Published doctoral dissertation, Eastern Michigan University, Ypsilanti, MI.

McNeece, A. (2019). *Launching and consolidating unstoppable learning.* Bloomington, IN: Solution Tree Press.

Melville, H. (1967). *Moby-Dick.* New York: Bantam Dell. (Original work published 1851)

Methe, S. A., & Hintze, J. M. (2003). Evaluating teacher modeling as a strategy to increase student reading behavior. *School Psychology Review, 32*(4), 617–623.

Meyer, S. (2005). *Twilight*. New York: Little, Brown and Company.

Michigan Association of Intermediate School Administrators. (2017). *Essential practices in early and elementary literacy*. Accessed at https://memspa.org/wp-content/uploads/2017/10 /Booklet-FINAL-9.14.17.pdf on October 29, 2019.

Mikami, A. Y., Ruzek, E. A., Hafen, C. A., Gregory, A., & Allen, J. P. (2017). Perceptions of relatedness with classroom peers promote adolescents' behavioral engagement and achievement in secondary school. *Journal of Youth and Adolescence, 46*(11), 2341–2354.

Miller, C. C. (2018). Does teacher diversity matter in student learning? *The New York Times*. Accessed at www.nytimes.com/2018/09/10/upshot/teacher-diversity-effect-students -learning.html on September 3, 2019.

Mindset Works. (n.d.). *How parents can instill a growth mindset at home*. Accessed at www .mindsetworks.com/parents/growth-mindset-parenting on April 19, 2019.

Moorman, E. A., & Pomerantz, E. M. (2010). Ability mindsets influence the quality of mothers' involvement in children's learning: An experimental investigation. *Developmental Psychology, 46*(5), 1354–1362.

Moreno, K. A. (2018). *Stem educators' integration of formative assessment in teaching and lesson design*. Published doctoral dissertation, College of Saint Elizabeth, Morristown, NJ.

Muhammad, A. (2009). *Transforming school culture: How to overcome staff division*. Bloomington, IN: Solution Tree Press.

Muhammad, A. (2015). *Overcoming the achievement gap trap: Liberating mindsets to effect change*. Bloomington, IN: Solution Tree Press.

Muhammad, A. (2018). *Transforming school culture: How to overcome staff division* (2nd ed.). Bloomington, IN: Solution Tree Press.

Muhammad, A., & Hollie, S. (2012). *The will to lead, the skill to teach: Transforming schools at every level*. Bloomington, IN: Solution Tree Press.

Murphy, K. (2014, May 16). Psst. Look over here. *The New York Times*. Accessed at www .nytimes.com/2014/05/17/sunday-review/the-eyes-have-it.html on June 14, 2019.

Musu, L. (2019, February 20). *A slightly more diverse public school teaching workforce* [Blog post]. Accessed at https://nces.ed.gov/blogs/nces/post/a-slightly-more-diverse-public -school-teaching-force on September 3, 2019.

National Center on Safe Supportive Learning Environments. (n.d.). *Protective factors*. Accessed at https://safesupportivelearning.ed.gov/training-technical-assistance/education-level /early-learning/protective-factors on June 2, 2019.

National Governors Association Center for Best Practices & Council of Chief State School Officers. (2010a). *Common Core State Standards for English language arts and literacy in history/social studies, science, and technical subjects*. Washington, DC: Author. Accessed at www.corestandards.org/assets/CCSSI_ELA%20Standards.pdf on April 10, 2019.

National Governors Association Center for Best Practices & Council of Chief State School Officers. (2010b). *Common Core State Standards for mathematics.* Washington, DC: Author. Accessed at www.corestandards.org/assets/CCSSI_Math%20Standards.pdf on April 10, 2019.

National Survey of Student Engagement. (2006). *Engaged learning for all students: Annual report 2006.* Accessed at http://nsse.iub.edu/NSSE_2006_Annual_Report/docs/NSSE _2006_Annual_Report.pdf on September 4, 2019.

National Survey of Student Engagement. (2013). *NSSE's conceptual framework.* Accessed at http://nsse.indiana.edu/html/conceptual_framework_2013.cfm on June 11, 2019.

Ng, C., Bartlett, B., & Elliott, S. N. (2018). *Empowering engagement: Creating learning opportunities for students from challenging backgrounds.* New York: Springer.

NGSS Lead States. (2013). *Next Generation Science Standards: For states, by states.* Washington, DC: National Academies Press.

Niemiec, C. P., & Ryan, R. M. (2009). Autonomy, competence, and relatedness in the classroom. *Theory and Research in Education, 7*(2), 133–144.

Nuthall, G. (1999). The way students learn: Acquiring knowledge from an integrated science and social studies unit. *Elementary School Journal, 99*(4), 303–341.

Nuthall, G., & Alton-Lee, A. (1995). Assessing classroom learning: How students use their knowledge and experience to answer classroom achievement test questions in science and social studies. *American Educational Research Journal, 32*(1), 185–223.

O'Toole, N., & Due, C. (2015). School engagement for academically at-risk students: A participatory research project. *The Australian Educational Researcher, 42*(1), 1–17.

Orkin, M., Pott, M., Wolf, M., May, S., & Brand, E. (2018). Beyond gold stars: Improving the skills and engagement of struggling readers through intrinsic motivation. *Reading & Writing Quarterly, 34*(3), 203–217.

Ortega, L., Malmberg, L., & Sammons, P. (2018). Teacher effects on Chilean children's achievement growth: A cross-classified multiple membership accelerated growth curve model. *Educational Evaluation and Policy Analysis, 40*(3), 473–501.

Orthner, D. K., Jones-Sanpei, H., Akis, P., & Rose, R. A. (2012). Improving middle school student engagement through career-relevant instruction in the core curriculum. *Journal of Educational Research, 106*(1), 27–38.

Parish, P. (1963). *Amelia Bedelia.* New York: Harper & Row.

Parker, P. D., Schoon, I., Tsai, Y., Nagy, G., Trautwein, U., & Eccles, J. (2012). Achievement, agency, gender, and socioeconomic background as predictors of postschool choices: A multi-context study. *Developmental Psychology, 48*(6), 1629–1642.

Parsons, S. A., Nuland, L. R., & Parsons, A. W. (2014). The ABCs of student engagement. *Phi Delta Kappan, 95*(8), 23–27.

Peterson, K. D., & Deal, T. E. (2009). *The shaping school culture fieldbook* (2nd ed.). San Francisco: Jossey-Bass.

Pettigrew, T. F., & Tropp, L. R. (2006). A meta-analytic test of intergroup contact theory. *Journal of Personality and Social Psychology, 90*(5), 751–783.

Pierson, R. (2013, May). *Every kid needs a champion* [Video file]. Accessed at www.ted.com /talks/rita_pierson_every_kid_needs_a_champion on August 30, 2019.

Pintrich, P. R., Smith, D. A. F., García, T., & McKeachie, W. J. (1991). *A manual for the use of the Motivated Strategies for Learning questionnaire.* Ann Arbor: MI: National Center for Research to Improve Postsecondary Teaching and Learning.

Polacco, P. (1994). *Mrs. Katz and Tush.* New York: Bantam Books.

Porosoff, L., & Weinstein, J. (2020). *Two-for-one teaching: Connecting instruction to student values.* Bloomington, IN: Solution Tree Press.

Powell, S. D. (2011). Wayside teaching: Building autonomy. *Middle School Journal (J3), 43*(2), 38–40.

Provini, C. (2017). *First-day-of-school surveys: Get to know students.* Accessed at www .educationworld.com/a_curr/back-to-school-student-survey-questionnaire.shtml on April 19, 2019.

Ratner, B. (2009). Pythagoras: Everyone knows his famous theorem, but not who discovered it 1000 years before him. *Journal of Targeting, Measurement and Analysis for Marketing, 17*(3), 229–242.

Rebell, M. A. (2017). *The schools' neglected mission: Preparing all students for civic participation.* New York: Center for Educational Equity. Accessed at www.centerforeducationalequity. org/publications/preparation-for-civic-participation/PCP-white-paper-summary_12-1-17. pdf on May 30, 2019.

Reeve, J. (2012). A self-determination theory perspective on student engagement. In S. L. Christenson, A. L. Reschly, & C. Wylie (Eds.), *Handbook of research on student engagement* (pp. 149–172). Boston: Springer.

Reeve, J., & Halusic, M. (2009). How K–12 teachers can put self-determination theory principles into practice. *Theory and Research in Education, 7*(2), 145–154.

Reeve, J., & Jang, H. (2006). What teachers say and do to support students' autonomy during a learning activity. *Journal of Educational Psychology, 98*(1), 209–218.

Reynolds-Keefer, L. (2010). Rubric-referenced assessment in teacher preparation: An opportunity to learn by using. *Practical Assessment, Research & Evaluation, 15*(8), 1–9.

Rimm-Kaufman, S. E., Baroody, A. E., Larsen, R. A. A., Curby, T. W., & Abry, T. (2015). To what extent do teacher-student interaction quality and student gender contribute to fifth graders' engagement in mathematics learning? *Journal of Educational Psychology, 107*(1), 170–185.

Roberson, R. (2013). *Helping students find relevance.* Accessed at www.apa.org/ed/precollege /ptn/2013/09/students-relevance on June 17, 2019.

Robertson, T. (n.d.). *The effects of autonomy on job satisfaction.* Accessed at http://work.chron .com/effects-autonomy-job-satisfaction-14677.html on April 19, 2019.

Robinson, K. (2009). *The element: How finding your passion changes everything.* New York: Viking.

Rolland, R. G. (2012). Synthesizing the evidence on classroom goal structures in middle and secondary schools: A meta-analysis and narrative review. *Review of Educational Research, 82*(4), 396–435.

Romine, W., Sadler, T. D., Presley, M., & Klosterman, M. L. (2014). Student interest in technology and science (SITS) survey: Development, validation, and use of a new instrument. *International Journal of Science and Mathematics Education, 12*(2), 261–283.

Rubin, R. (2012). Independence, disengagement, and discipline. *Reclaiming Children and Youth, 21*(1), 42–45.

Rumberger, R. W. (2011). *Dropping out: Why students drop out of high school and what can be done about it.* Cambridge, MA: Harvard University Press.

Ryan, R. M., & Deci, E. L. (2000a). Intrinsic and extrinsic motivations: Classic definitions and new directions. *Contemporary Educational Psychology, 25*(1), 54–67.

Ryan, R. M., & Deci, E. L. (2000b). Self-determination theory and the facilitation of intrinsic motivation, social development, and well-being. *American Psychologist, 55*(1), 68–78.

Ryan, R. M., & Deci, E. L. (2009). Promoting self-determined school engagement: Motivation, learning, and well-being. In K. R. Wentzel & A. Wigfield (Eds.), *Handbook of motivation at school* (pp. 171–196). New York: Routledge.

Sabatier, G. (2019). *5 rappers on personal finance.* Accessed at https://millennialmoney.com /rappers-personal-finance on October 29, 2019.

Sadler, D. R. (1989). Formative assessment and the design of instructional systems. *Instructional Science, 18*(2), 119–144.

Saeed, S., & Zyngier, D. (2012). How motivation influences student engagement: A qualitative case study. *Journal of Education and Learning, 1*(2), 252–267.

Sanders, W. L., & Rivers, J. C. (1996). *Cumulative and residual effects of teachers on future student academic achievement.* Knoxville, TN: University of Tennessee Value-Added Research and Assessment Center.

Schaps, E. (2005). The role of supportive school environments in promoting academic success. In *Getting results, developing safe and healthy kids update 5: Student health, supportive schools, and academic success* (pp. 37–56). Sacramento: California Department of Education Press.

Scharf, A. (2014). *Critical practices for anti-bias education.* Accessed at www.tolerance.org /sites/default/files/Critical%20Practicesv4_final.pdf on June 16, 2019.

Schein, E. H. (2010). *Organizational culture and leadership* (4th ed.). San Francisco: Jossey-Bass.

Schilling, J. C. (2009). *A quantitative and qualitative investigation of variability and contextual sources related to the academic engagement of minority and economically disadvantaged adolescents.* Published doctoral dissertation, University of Virginia, Charlottesville.

Schmidt, J., Shah, P., Vedantam, S., Boyle, T., Penman, M., & Nesterak, M. (2019). Creative differences: The benefits of reaching out to people unlike ourselves. *NPR.* Accessed at www.npr.org/2019/01/24/687707404/creative-differences-the-benefits-of-reaching-out -to-people-unlike-ourselves on September 3, 2019.

Schmoker, M. J. (2011). *Focus: Elevating the essentials to radically improve student learning.* Alexandria, VA: Association for Supervision and Curriculum Development.

Schunk, D. H., & Mullen, C. A. (2012). Self-efficacy as an engaged learner. In S. L. Christenson, A. L. Reschly, & C. Wylie (Eds.), *Handbook of research on student engagement* (pp. 219–235). Boston: Springer.

Schussler, D. L. (2009). Beyond content: How teachers manage classrooms to facilitate intellectual engagement for disengaged students. *Theory Into Practice, 48*(2), 114–121.

Schweinle, A., Turner, J. C., & Meyer, D. K. (2009). Understanding young adolescents' optimal experiences in academic settings. *Journal of Experimental Education, 77*(2), 125–143.

Schwinger, M., Wirthwein, L., Lemmer, G., & Steinmayr, R. (2014). Academic self-handicapping and achievement: A meta-analysis. *Journal of Educational Psychology, 106*(3), 744–761.

Scott, M. (2019). *Why it's important to apologize.* Accessed at www.verywellmind.com/the -importance-of-apologizing-3144986 on July 29, 2019.

Seaton, M., Parker, P., Marsh, H. W., Craven, R. G., & Yeung, A. S. (2014). The reciprocal relations between self-concept, motivation and achievement: Juxtaposing academic self-concept and achievement goal orientations for mathematics success. *Educational Psychology, 34*(1), 49–72.

Shakespeare, W. (1974). Henry IV, part 2. In G. B. Evans, H. Levin, H. Baker, A. Barton, F. Kermode, H. Smith, M. Edel, & C. H. Shattuck (Eds.), *The riverside Shakespeare* (pp. 886–929). Boston: Houghton Mifflin. (Original work published 1600)

Shakespeare, W. (1997). A midsummer night's dream. In G. B. Evans & J. J. M. Tobin (Eds.), *The riverside Shakespeare* (2nd ed., Vol. 1, pp. 251–283). Boston: Houghton Mifflin. (Original work published 1600)

Shavelson, R. J., Hubner, J. J., & Stanton, G. C. (1976). Self-concept: Validation of construct interpretations. *Review of Educational Research, 46*(3), 407–441.

Sheffield, A. N. (2017). *Autonomy support: Teacher beliefs and practices during STEAM instruction and its influence on elementary students.* Published doctoral dissertation, University of Alabama, Tuscaloosa. Accessed at https://ir.ua.edu/bitstream/handle/123456789/3560 /file_1.pdf?sequence=1&isAllowed=y on August 26, 2019.

Skinner, E. A., & Belmont, M. J. (1993). Motivation in the classroom: Reciprocal effects of teacher behavior and student engagement across the school year. *Journal of Educational Psychology, 85*(4), 571–581.

Skinner, E. A., Kindermann, T. A., Connell, J. P., & Wellborn, J. G. (2009). Engagement and disaffection as organizational constructs in the dynamics of motivational development. In K. R. Wentzel & A. Wigfield (Eds.), *Handbook of motivation at school* (pp. 223–246). New York: Routledge.

Skinner, E. A., & Pitzer, J. R. (2012). Developmental dynamics of student engagement, coping, and everyday resilience. In S. L. Christenson, A. L. Reschly, & C. Wylie (Eds.), *Handbook of research on student engagement* (pp. 21–44). New York: Springer.

Skinner, E. A., Pitzer, J. R., & Steele, J. S. (2016). Can student engagement serve as a motivational resource for academic coping, persistence, and learning during late elementary and early middle school? *Developmental Psychology, 52*(12), 2099–2117.

Sloan, D. (n.d.). *Reflection activities: Tried and true teaching methods to enhance students' service-learning experience.* Accessed at www.usf.edu/engagement/documents/s-l -reflection-activities.pdf on April 19, 2019.

Smith, K. C. (2019). *Developing a culturally relevant curriculum and breaking the barriers of cognitive and cultural dissonance.* Published doctoral dissertation, Wayne State University, Detroit, MI. Accessed at https://digitalcommons.wayne.edu/oa_dissertations/2187 on September 4, 2019.

Snipes, J., & Tran, L. (2017). *Growth mindset, performance avoidance, and academic behaviors in Clark County School District* (REL 2017–226). Washington, DC: Institute of Education Sciences.

Soiferman, L. K. (2015). *Understanding the effectiveness of rubrics from the students' point of view.* Accessed at https://files.eric.ed.gov/fulltext/ED558553.pdf on April 19, 2019.

Spiegel, A. (2012). Teachers' expectations can influence how students perform. *NPR.* Accessed at www.npr.org/sections/health-shots/2012/09/18/161159263/teachers -expectations-can-influence-how-students-perform on August 30, 2019.

Stand Together Foundation. (2017). *The cycle of educational failure and poverty.* Accessed at www.stand-together.org/cycle-educational-failure on May 30, 2019.

StateUniversity.com. (n.d.). *Peer relations and learning.* Accessed at https://education .stateuniversity.com/pages/2315/Peer-Relations-Learning.html on June 11, 2019.

Statistics Canada. (2015). *Table A.11: Graduation rate, Canada, provinces and territories, 2005/2006 to 2009/2010.* Accessed at www150.statcan.gc.ca/n1/pub/81-595-m /2011095/tbl/tbla.11-eng.htm on April 19, 2019.

Steele, D. M., & Cohn-Vargas, B. (2013). *Identity safe classrooms: Places to belong and learn.* Thousand Oaks, CA: SAGE.

Stefanou, C. R., Perencevich, K. C., DiCintio, M., & Turner, J. C. (2004). Supporting autonomy in the classroom: Ways teachers encourage student decision making and ownership. *Educational Psychologist, 39*(2), 97–110.

Strauss, V. (2017). It puts kids to sleep—but teachers keep lecturing anyway. Here's what to do about it. *The Washington Post.* Accessed at www.washingtonpost.com/news/answer -sheet/wp/2017/07/11/it-puts-kids-to-sleep-but-teachers-keep-lecturing-anyway-heres -what-to-do-about-it/?utm_term=.038f832876a2 on June 10, 2019.

Strutchens, M. E. (1999). Data collection: Getting to know your students' attitudes. *Mathematics Teaching in the Middle School, 4*(6), 382–384.

Stubrich, G. (1993). The fifth discipline: The art and practice of the learning organization. *Columbia Journal of World Business, 28*(2), 108–109.

Suttie, J. (2016). *Four ways teachers can reduce implicit bias.* Accessed at https://greatergood .berkeley.edu/article/item/four_ways_teachers_can_reduce_implicit bias on June 16, 2019.

Svab, H., & Miltenberger, T. (1995). Integrating communication and social skills using ensemble techniques. In G. Duquette (Ed.), *Second language practice: Classroom strategies for developing communicative competence* (pp. 55–66). Clevedon, England: Multilingual Matters.

Tate, M. L. (2010). *Worksheets don't grow dendrites: 20 instructional strategies that engage the brain* (2nd ed.). Thousand Oaks, CA: SAGE.

Thompson, M., & Thompson, J. (2009). *Transforming standards into learning, version 7.* Marion, NC: Learning Focused.

Tomlinson, C. A., & Imbeau, M. B. (2010). *Leading and managing a differentiated classroom.* Alexandria, VA: Association for Supervision and Curriculum Development.

Troyer, M. (2017). A mixed-methods study of adolescents' motivation to read. *Teachers College Record, 119*(5), 1–48.

Tsai, Y., Kunter, M., Ludtke, O., Trautwein, U., & Ryan, R. M. (2008). What makes lessons interesting? The role of situational and individual factors in three school subjects. *Journal of Educational Psychology, 100*(2), 460–472.

Tucker, O. G. (2018). Positive teacher influence strategies to improve secondary instrumental students' motivation and perceptions of self. *Update: Applications of Research in Music Education, 36*(3), 5–11.

Turcotte, S., & Hamel, C. (2016). Using scaffold supports to improve student practice and understanding of an authentic inquiry process in science. *Canadian Journal of Science, Mathematics and Technology Education, 16*(1), 77–91.

Turner, V. E. (2017). *Learning environments in mathematics*. Published doctoral dissertation, Brenau University, Gainesville, GA.

Ufer, S., Rach, S., & Kosiol, T. (2017). Interest in mathematics = Interest in mathematics? What general measures of interest reflect when the object of interest changes. *ZDM: The International Journal on Mathematics Education*, *49*(3), 397–409.

Umbach, P. D., & Wawrzynski, M. R. (2005). Faculty do matter: The role of college faculty in student learning and engagement. *Research in Higher Education*, *46*, 153–184.

Ure, C., & Gray, J. (2012). *Research and mapping for MCEECDYA Project: Student academic engagement*. Carlton South, Victoria, Australia: Standing Council on School Education and Early Childhood.

Urhahne, D. (2015). Teacher behavior as a mediator of the relationship between teacher judgment and students' motivation and emotion. *Teaching and Teacher Education*, *45*, 73–82.

Van Craeyevelt, S., Verschueren, K., Vancraeyveldt, C., Wouters, S., & Colpin, H. (2017). The role of preschool teacher-child interactions in academic adjustment: An intervention study with Playing-2-Gether. *British Journal of Educational Psychology*, *87*(3), 345–364.

Van den Berghe, L., Cardon, G., Tallir, I., Kirk, D., & Haerens, L. (2016). Dynamics of need-supportive and need-thwarting teaching behavior: The bidirectional relationship with student engagement and disengagement in the beginning of a lesson. *Physical Education and Sport Pedagogy*, *21*(6), 653–670.

Veríssimo, M., Torres, N., Silva, F., Fernandes, C., Vaughn, B. E., & Santos, A. J. (2017). Children's representations of attachment and positive teacher–child relationships. *Frontiers in Psychology*, *8*.

Vygotsky, L. S. (1978). *Mind in society: The development of higher psychological processes*. Cambridge, MA: Harvard University Press.

Vygotsky, L. S. (1987). *The collected works of L. S. Vygotsky: Volume 1, problems of general psychology, including the volume thinking and speech*. New York: Plenum Press. (Original work published 1934)

Waack, S. (n.d.). *Glossary of Hattie's influences on student achievement*. Accessed at https://visible-learning.org/glossary/ on April 19, 2019.

Wang, Z., Bergin, C., & Bergin, D. A. (2014). Measuring engagement in fourth to twelfth grade classrooms: The classroom engagement inventory. *School Psychology Quarterly*, *29*(4), 517–535.

Warner-Griffin, C., Cunningham, B. C., & Noel, A. (2018). *Public school teacher autonomy, satisfaction, job security, and commitment: 1999–2000 and 2011–12*. Accessed at https://nces.ed.gov/pubs2018/2018103.pdf on June 10, 2019.

Wehmeyer, M. L., Shogren, K. A., Toste, J. R., & Mahal, S. (2017). Self-determined learning to motivate struggling learners in reading and writing. *Intervention in School and Clinic, 52*(5), 295–303.

Wentzel, K. R. (1999). Social-motivational processes and interpersonal relationships: Implications for understanding motivation at school. *Journal of Educational Psychology, 91*(1), 76–97.

Whaley, K. A. (2012). Using students' interests as algebraic models. *Mathematics Teaching in the Middle School, 17*(6), 372–378.

Wiggins, G. (2012). Seven keys to effective feedback. *Educational Leadership, 70*(1), 10–16.

Wiggins, G., & McTighe, J. (2005). *Understanding by design* (Rev. ed.). Alexandria, VA: Association for Supervision and Curriculum Development.

Wijnen, M., Loyens, S. M. M., Wijnia, L., Smeets, G., Kroeze, M. J., & Van der Molen, H. T. (2018). Is problem-based learning associated with students' motivation? A quantitative and qualitative study. *Learning Environments Research, 21*(2), 173–193.

Williams, D. R., Brule, H., Kelley, S. S., & Skinner, E. A. (2018). Science in the learning gardens: A study of motivation, achievement, and science identity in low-income middle schools. *International Journal of STEM Education, 5*(8).

Wong, H. K., & Wong, R. T. (2001). *The first days of school: How to be an effective teacher.* Mountain View, CA: Harry K. Wong.

Wu, J. Y., Hughes. J. N., & Kwok, O. M. (2010). Teacher-student relationship quality type in elementary grades: Effects on trajectories for achievement and engagement. *Journal of School Psychology, 48*(5), 357–387.

X, M., & Haley, A. (1964). *The autobiography of Malcolm X.* New York: Ballantine.

Yale. (n.d.). *Creating and using rubrics.* Accessed at https://ctl.yale.edu/Rubrics on April 19, 2019.

Yeager, D. S., Purdie-Vaughns, V., Garcia, J., Apfel, N., Brzustoski, P., Master, A., et al. (2014). Breaking the cycle of mistrust: Wise interventions to provide critical feedback across the racial divide. *Journal of Experimental Psychology: General, 143*(2), 804–824.

Young, M. R. (2018). Reflection fosters deep learning: The 'reflection page & relevant to you' intervention. *Journal of Instructional Pedagogies, 20.*

Zwiers, J. (2014). *Building academic language: Meeting Common Core standards across disciplines, grades 5–12* (2nd ed.). Hoboken, NJ: Wiley.

INDEX

Launching and Consolidating Unstoppable Learning
Alexander McNeece
Adopted by educators worldwide, the Unstoppable Learning model includes seven elements of teaching and learning. This book offers strategies for two of the elements—*launching* (introducing content and hooking students) and *consolidating* (choosing what to do with instructional time).
BKF740

Fifty Strategies to Boost Cognitive Engagement
Rebecca Stobaugh
Transform your classroom from one of passive knowledge consumption to one of active engagement. In this well-researched book, Rebecca Stobaugh shares fifty strategies for building a thinking culture that emphasizes essential 21st century skills—from critical thinking and problem solving to teamwork and creativity.
BKF894

Making Learning Flow
John Spencer
Rethink student engagement and bring flow to the center of instruction to inspire students to love learning and reach new levels of achievement. Generate a state of flow in the classroom every day to spark optimal student performance.
BKF733

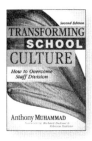

Transforming School Culture, Second Edition
Anthony Muhammad
The second edition of this best-selling resource delivers powerful new insight into the four types of educators and how to work with each group to create thriving schools. The book also includes Muhammad's latest research and a new chapter of frequently asked questions.
BKF793

a division of

Solution Tree | Press

Solution Tree

Visit SolutionTree.com or call 800.733.6786 to order.

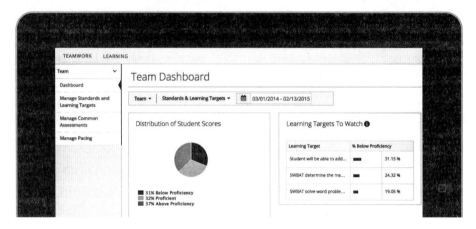